TRUE CRIME, TRUE NORTH

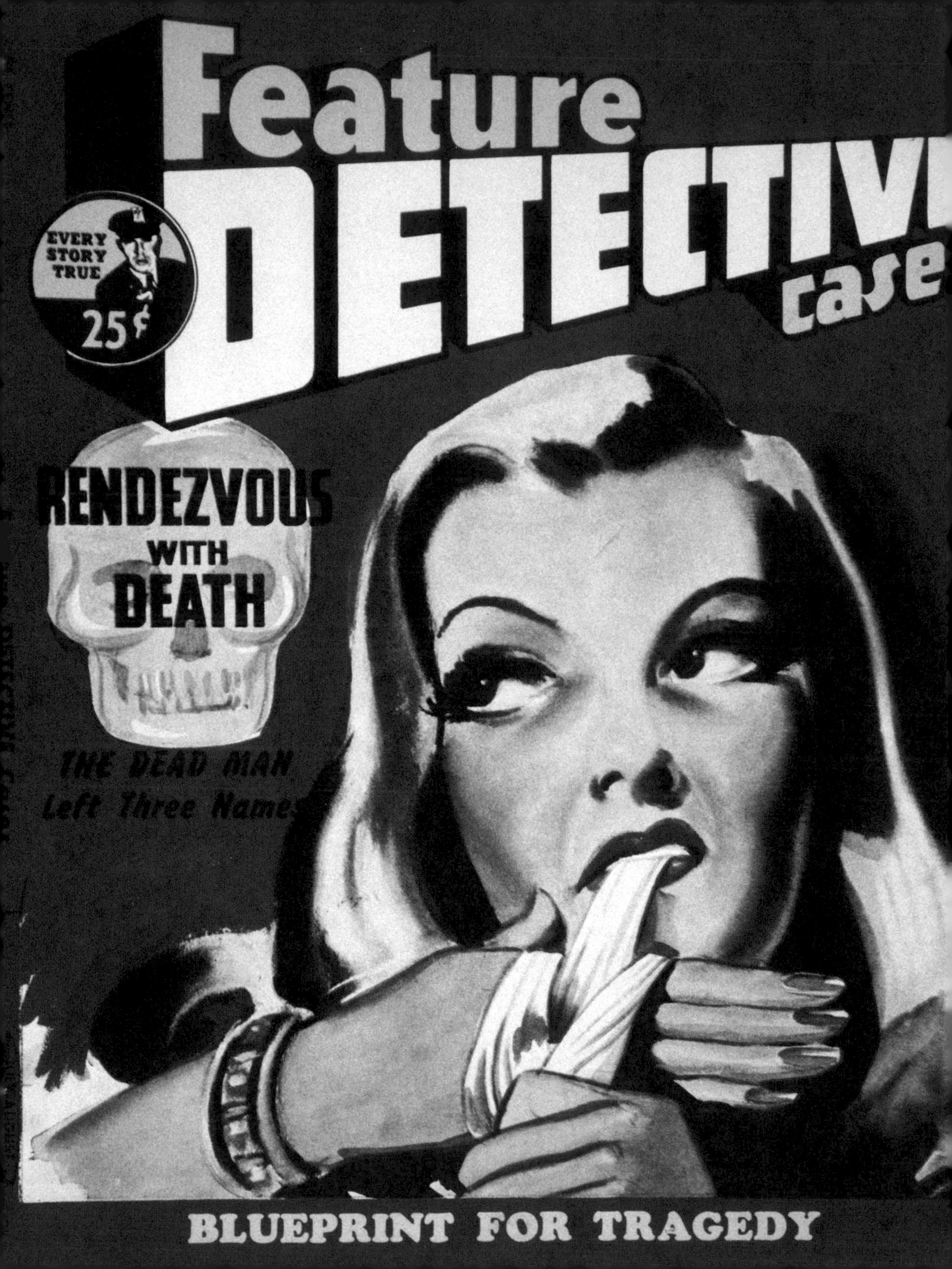

Feature
DETECTIV
case
EVERY STORY TRUE
25¢
RENDEZVOUS WITH DEATH
THE DEAD MAN Left Three Names
BLUEPRINT FOR TRAGEDY

TRUE CRIME, TRUE NORTH

THE GOLDEN AGE OF
CANADIAN PULP MAGAZINES

CAROLYN STRANGE AND TINA LOO

RAINCOAST BOOKS

Vancouver

Unless otherwise noted, all images contained in this book are from the National Library of Canada, Pulp Art Collection. All black and white photographs are B-movie stills found in the "Cheesecake Photos" file (see p. 25) contained in that collection.

Raincoast Books gratefully acknowledges the ongoing support of the Canada Council for the Arts; the British Columbia Arts Council; and the Government of Canada through the Department of Canadian Heritage Book Publishing Industry Development Program (BPIDP).

Raincoast Books
9050 Shaughnessy Street
Vancouver, British Columbia
Canada V6P 6E5
www.raincoast.com

In the United States:
Publishers Group West
1700 Fourth Street
Berkeley, California
USA 94710

National Library of Canada Cataloguing in Publication Data

Strange, Carolyn, 1959-
        True crime, true north: the golden age of Canadian pulp magazines / Carolyn Strange and Tina Loo.

Includes bibliographical references.
ISBN 1-55192-689-X

1. Crime—Canada–Periodicals. 2. Pulp literature—History and criticism.
3. Canadian periodicals—History—20th century. I. Loo, Tina Merrill, 1962-
II. Title.

PN4914.C74S77 2004   364.971'05   C2003-906748-3

Printed and bound in Canada.

1 2 3 4 5 6 7 8 9 10

TEXT AND COVER DESIGN: BILLY DOUGLAS @ THE BANG

CONTENTS

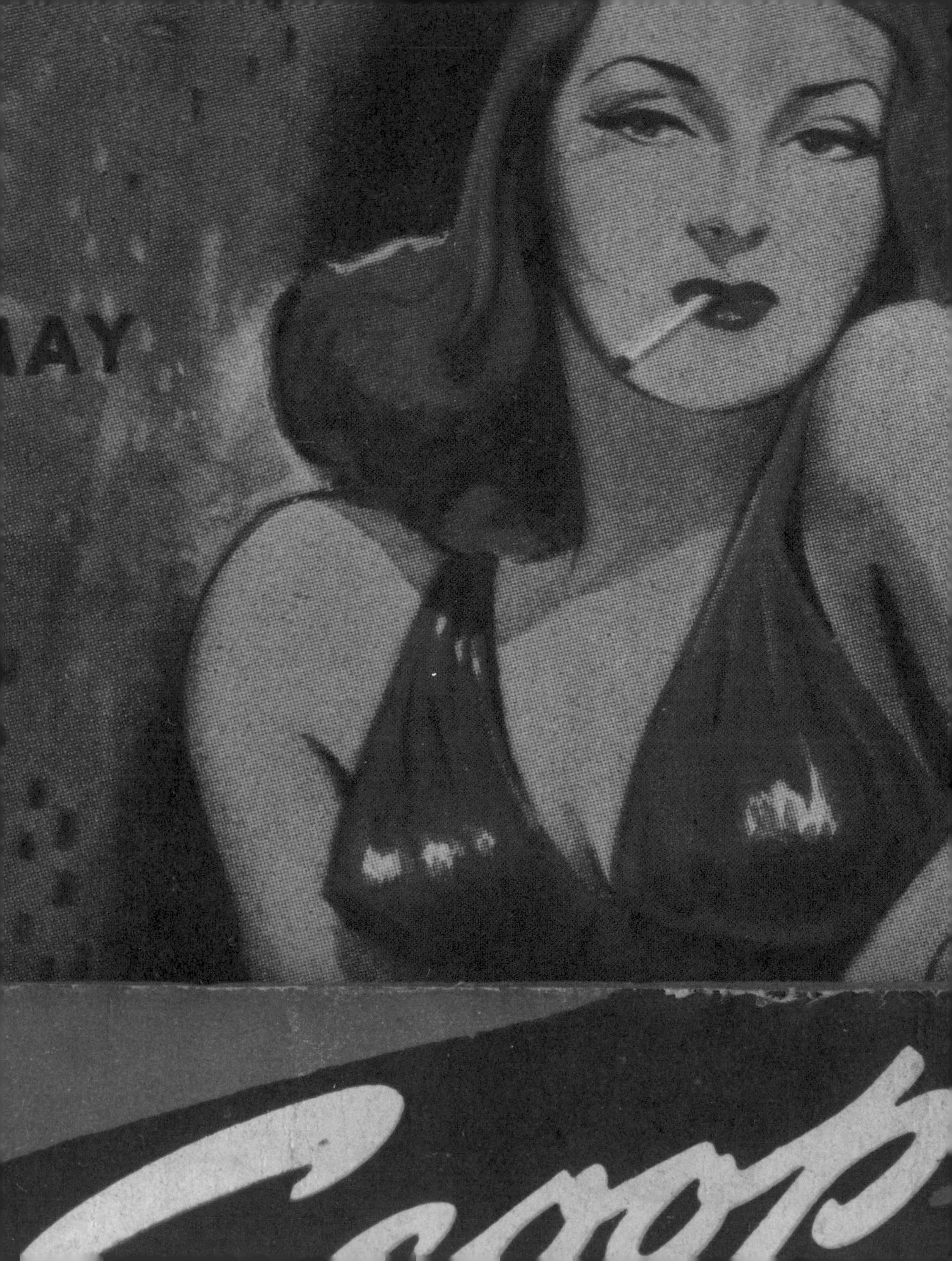

JULY

A *True Crime* MAGAZINE

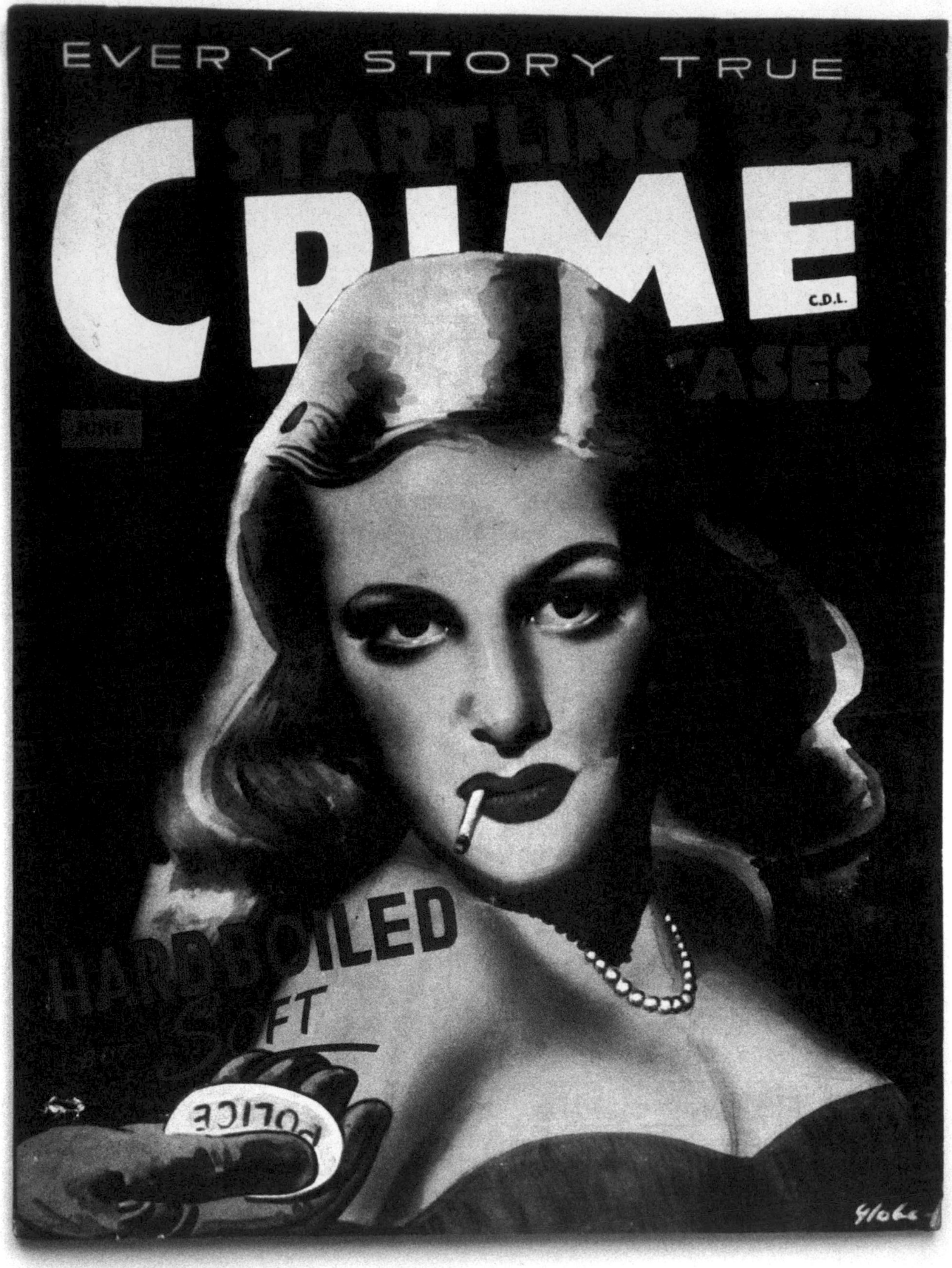
EVERY STORY TRUE
STARTLING
CRIME
C.D.L.
CASES

INTRODUCTION

THEIR COVERS ARE BOLD AND BRASSY, their advertisements are spicy and their stories are filled with violence and death. Who can resist pulp magazines?

Half a century before "reality television" gained vast viewing audiences, real-life criminal cases, most of them murders, found their way into another popular format: luridly illustrated true crime magazines. Their heyday was the 1940s, the decade when the Depression finally ended, only to launch North Americans into war. True crime pulps, along with radio plays and picture shows, were cheap diversions from troubles at home and abroad. They provided a bit of spice for servicemen travelling on trains and they gave women a few thrills on their coffee breaks. You didn't need a library card to read about daring murders and desperate manhunts — all you needed was a dime or two and a taste for crime.

Nowadays we're drawn to the pulps on account of their kitschy qualities; their reproduced covers (the more garish the better) adorn fridge magnets and campy calendars. Pulp magazines have become as emblematic of mid-20th-century American pop culture as Hollywood B movies and baseball cards. During the 1940s, however, a pulp-publishing industry briefly flourished north of the United States border, and true crime magazines with stories about Canadian murder cases began to hit city newsstands and rural railroad stations across the country. New Canadian magazines, such as *Daring Detective* and *True Police Cases* suddenly appeared, following the American model of wrapping stories about real murders, heists and rapes in dazzling sexy covers. Canadian pulp magazine editors continued to publish accounts of crimes committed in the U.S., but they also published stories about Canadian good guys and bad guys (and gals).

Prior to the 1940s Canadians had read about homegrown criminals in a variety of formats, including local newspapers and scandal sheets, classier book collections (such as Murders and Mysteries) and a genre of dime novels known as "Northerns." Like Westerns with their stress on man-size adventures, they were uniquely Canadian because they specialized in regional crimes (Canada's Arctic) and regional crime fighters (Mounties). By the mid-20th century, true crime magazines provided a cheaper, slimmer and newly seductive package for similar stories, based on murders committed and solved in Canada.

The true crime pulps combined factual detail, gleaned from court reports and police files, with romantic depictions of ruthless killers and manly lawmen. They were significantly lower in price than hardcover books about famous crimes and criminals, and they were far more colourful, at least on the outside. While stories of Canada's Far North remained a staple, readers could also tuck into stories about murderers captured by Vancouver detectives or Montreal cops. From the Arctic to big-city alleyways, Canadian pulps covered the national crime beat and did it with pizzazz.

WHAT'S IN A STORY?

Novelists like Dashiell Hammett and James M. Cain were limited only by their imaginations when they wrote crime fiction in the 1940s; in contrast, true crime writers were stuck with events that had actually occurred. They wrote for magazines that appeared with the bold endorsement: "TRUE FACTS FROM OFFICIAL FILES." But that didn't mean that true crime writers picked just any sort of case to write up, and it didn't mean that editors were willing to pay for just any kind of story. In fact, there were certain conventions that writers had to follow if they wanted to turn true crime into cold cash.

Writers wrote about crimes that interested them, of course, but what interested them most were cases with selling power. Prior to the 1940s they had sold only to American and British publishers, but the market changed suddenly in 1940, thanks to a Canadian government move designed to preserve the country's balance of trade with the United States. Prime Minister Mackenzie King's Liberals imposed an importation ban on a wide range of nonessential goods, including chocolate, champagne and playing cards. The

War Exchange Conservation Act (1940) also banned the importation of pulp magazines, specifically periodicals featuring "detective, sex, western and alleged true or confession stories." Canadian publishers, who had previously distributed cheap books and produced comic books and scandal sheets, found themselves with a ready market and an opportunity to profit by adding pulp magazines to their rosters.

The act allowed Canadian writers to continue selling stories to U.S. publishers (and many of the more prolific, such as Philip Godsell and C. V. Tench, did), but it also widened the market for stories about Canadian crimes. As the flow of cheap American magazines dried up, Canadian publishers scrambled to meet the demand for the pulps. By the early 1940s Toronto operations such as Superior Publishers and Daring Productions transformed Canada from a net consumer of pulp magazines to a net producer. This period was well before the era in which publishers were pushed to promote "Canadian content"; in fact, pulp editors of the 1940s were happy to rely on submissions from U.S. authors, or pirated copies of stories published in U.S. magazines. But Canadian publishers were also prepared to accept stories about local crimes, submitted by writers stationed in Canada.

The two most prominent publishers, Toronto's Al Valentine and brothers Lou and Moe Ruby, had a clear idea of what it took to publish a true crime magazine in Canada — essentially a package that mimicked the "pepped-up character" of U.S. detective magazines without attracting the ire of Canadian censors. Publishers' calls for submissions were quite broad: "Any type of crime case that would make a thrilling story." Yet an examination of the published stories confirms that Canadian true crime pulp editors were willing to accept only those murder cases with dramatic angles that writers could play to the hilt. True crime followed certain stylistic and moral conventions in the 1940s. In the pulps, readers followed the trail that lawmen pursued to track down criminals; indeed, every story turned on the hunt and every killer, no matter how smart, left a trail, whether it was a bloody shoe print or a pair of silk panties. Stories that made it into print were short on legal fine points and character complexity and long on police pursuits. The moral of the story was ultimately the same: no one could expect to get away with murder.

Thrilling true-crime stories weren't ready-made — they had to be fashioned into pulp material, first through research. Writers learned about cases the same way the public did, through the crime pages in their local newspapers. Some, like the writers for Lou Ruby's cynical, wisecracking *True Police Cases,* had a head start since they held day jobs as reporters for Toronto's

LETTER TO THE EDITOR

Producing a true crime story was a matter of applying "technique," fiddling with chronology to build tension, and telling the story from a law-and-order perspective. But it wasn't easy to fashion a ripping tale when the outcome was always conviction and hanging. As Miss Violet Marken complained to the editor of <u>Dare Devil Detective</u>, there was nothing worse than a predictable true crime story: "I did not like the story entitled 'Death at the Dam,'" she wrote. "The crooks ... are all very nasty and unscrupulous. The good guys and girls save the father and the dam and the girl, and everything worth saving."

dailies and tabloids. For these writers, selling the odd story to a true crime magazine netted them a little moonlighting money. Others, like Philip Godsell (former Hudson's Bay Company employee and subsequently auditor for Canadian Pacific Airlines), or Vancouver high school history teacher W. W. Bride, sold their work to Ruby's rival Al Valentine, whose stable of publications included *Factual Detective* and *Scoop Detective*. But even these writers

FACTUAL
DETECTIVE
C.D.C.
STORIES
LAFF
TERROR IN THE SANITARIUM
TRUE CRIME CASES
TRAPPED by the LIE DETECTOR
Plunder of the BANK-CRACKING BEAUTY

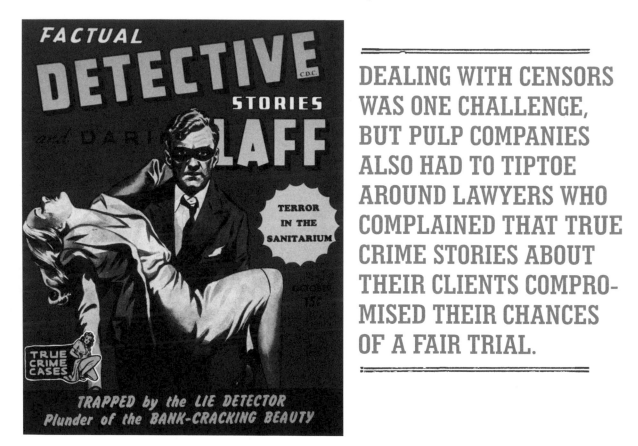

DEALING WITH CENSORS WAS ONE CHALLENGE, BUT PULP COMPANIES ALSO HAD TO TIPTOE AROUND LAWYERS WHO COMPLAINED THAT TRUE CRIME STORIES ABOUT THEIR CLIENTS COMPROMISED THEIR CHANCES OF A FAIR TRIAL.

knew it was best to cultivate relationships with crime beat reporters, as well as police officers and lawyers, if they were ever to get the chance to scoop a hot case.

In the 1940s the lawman's view of crime and criminals prevailed in the Canadian pulps: there were no unsolved mysteries or bungled cases, and no instances where criminals failed to get their just desserts. For instance, one magazine editor rejected a Godsell manuscript concerning an Inuit man who went unpunished for killing a group of American scientists. "No amount of explaining could fix that with the readers to make them believe that the

Eskimos were justified in killing a man who was sleeping," the editor insisted. But he went on to make a broader point about the moral code of 1940s true crime: "It is rather difficult to justify murder anyhow … and when no punishment whatsoever follows, then we have to figure out a way to overcome it." More often than not that meant sticking to stories of eye-for-an-eye justice — not at the hands of American-style vigilantes, but of Canada's police and courts.

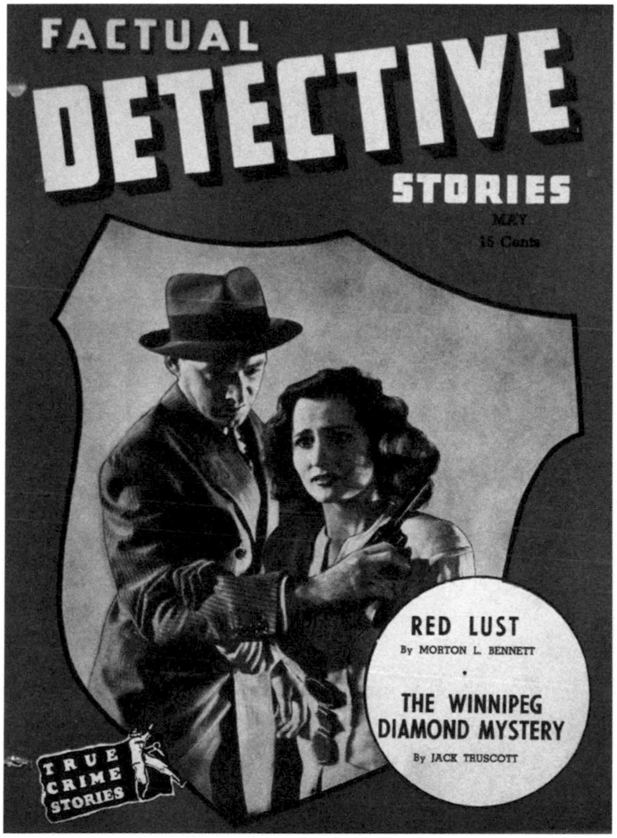
FACTUAL
DETECTIVE
STORIES
MAY
15 Cents
RED LUST
By MORTON L. BENNETT
THE WINNIPEG DIAMOND MYSTERY
By JACK TRUSCOTT
TRUE CRIME STORIES

Given these editorial expectations, law enforcement officers were the unquestioned heroes in every story. And every hero needs a villain. In true crime the criminals sometimes had certain admirable qualities, such as skill or daring, but writers knew that editors expected them to portray villains as the authors of their own misfortune. When one manuscript offered shades of grey in its moral evaluation of a Yukon outlaw, the pulp editor insisted on changes. "It should be explained plainly," he chided, "that [the criminal's] apparent fight for law and order was a blind — that he was in fact a ruthless crook and this outward show was simply a means to a criminal end." Bad guys were bad through and through: there was no room for moral ambiguity or antiheroes in a period when the Allies were fighting supreme evil. In the midcentury world of Canadian true crime, deadly deeds always sprang from individual criminals' deadly sins (envy, anger, pride, avarice or lust).

Making every lawbreaker conform to the stereotype of the true crime villain wasn't just a literary technique; it also was a legal requirement. Pulp publishers self-policed their content or tried to dodge the scrutiny of Canadian censors. In fact, Al Valentine moved into the pulp-publishing business after Moe Ruby asked the then printer to produce an issue of his scandal sheet, *The Tattler*, for distribution in Buffalo, because the Rubys were facing indecency charges in Canada. Editors who wanted to distribute in Canada constantly reminded writers that references to "loose women" and "the so-called sacrilegious element" (meaning anything the least bit critical of Christianity) could bring unwelcome heat. So could any profanity. As a result, the dialogue in 1940s Canadian pulps sounds stilted and even childish to our ears, something that irked writers of the day, as well. As Godsell griped, publishers' fears of indecency charges meant his "hard-boiled rough-necks [had] to say 'Goodness!' instead of 'Damn!'"

Dealing with censors was one challenge, but pulp companies also had to tiptoe around lawyers who complained that true crime stories about their clients compromised their chances of a fair trial. In order to avoid lawsuits, magazine editors waited until trials closed before they published stories. And they went a step further by substituting fictitious names to protect witnesses who got mixed up in murders. Using untrue names was one of the accepted practices in the true crime business.

If writers could find good cases, master the narrative technique and steer clear of censors they could expect a tidy profit from stories. Rates varied, but in the 1940s it was common for companies such as Pastime or Fireside Publications to offer authors between $250 and $400 for an original story, and $50 to $75 for ones that had appeared before (sometimes altering nothing but the title, or substituting a writer's pseudonym). Good stories had long lives, especially if writers could tempt U.S. publishers such as Dell and King Features Syndicate. The most successful managed to pitch their Canadian products to Britain, Australia and South Africa, where readers were already primed by Northerns and the talkies for murders committed in the remote North, solved by heroic Mounties.

Back on home ground a wider range of cases, including murders committed in Canada's unsettled west and its biggest cities, sold in the Canadian pulps. Thanks to the U.S. importation ban, nationwide distribution networks such as Ontario News and Sinnet developed to spread stories of local murders to readers across the country. Following the "technique," Canadian true crime stories chronicled the police chase, skipped quickly through the trial and moved toward its inevitable outcome: the guilty verdict, which restored social harmony and reset moral values. The cases that best conveyed these values were ones in which Canadian killers had paid with their lives (most at the end of the hangman's noose, but some with guns a-blazing, and the odd one taking the coward's way out).

BAD MEN AND BAD PLACES

If true crime narratives were formulaic, the characters in the pulps were barely more than cardboard cut-outs. Racial, ethnic and gender stereotypes allowed writers to sketch the types of men or women involved in cases without wasting too many words. Even a sturdy Briton's criminal tendencies could be outlined with remarks about his facial disfigurement or odd gait. True crime writers turned to prevailing prejudices about non-Anglo people's immorality and amorality. And everybody knew that women came in two types only: victims and vixens.

Racial profiling wasn't a dirty term in the 1940s pulps; in every story race provided a shorthand explanation for certain sorts of people's purported propensity to commit certain types of crimes. Anglo-Canadians and Northern Europeans were smart and cool-headed in the pulps (unless addled by drink or maddened by temptresses); Southern and Eastern Europeans and francophones were brutish and lusty; Americans were greedy and sharp; and Native peoples were prone to be passionate and uncivilized. While most stories explored the underbelly of Canada's colonial legacies and its more recent immigration trends, cases involving Asian or black victims or perpetrators were rarities. Pulp writers pandered to English Canadians' anti-Native prejudices and fears of European "foreigners," but they simultaneously reassured readers that law and order Canadian-style was there, ready to right any and every wrong.

The true crime writers were just as prone to play up stereotypical crime scenes and settings. Using this hoary story-writing convention allowed them to indulge in a little literary licence, coding Canadian regions with moral meanings. The Far North and the remote West were places of adventure in tourism and travel literature, but in the pulps they were Canada's barely civilized zones, where whites reverted to savagery and Native criminality flourished. Far from cooling tempers, the Canadian environment *induced* such violence, as one story warned: "When blood runs hot in the north country, murder born of passion must be avenged." The nation's cities and rural communities, however, had their dark sides, too. Depictions of seedy hotel rooms, lonely farmhouses and dark winter streets (clichés lifted from Gothic novels, crime fiction and film noir) always signalled that something nasty was bound to happen to some hapless victim.

Drawing rooms and vicarages might have provided stock settings for polite crime fiction writers such as Agatha Christie, but respectable settings

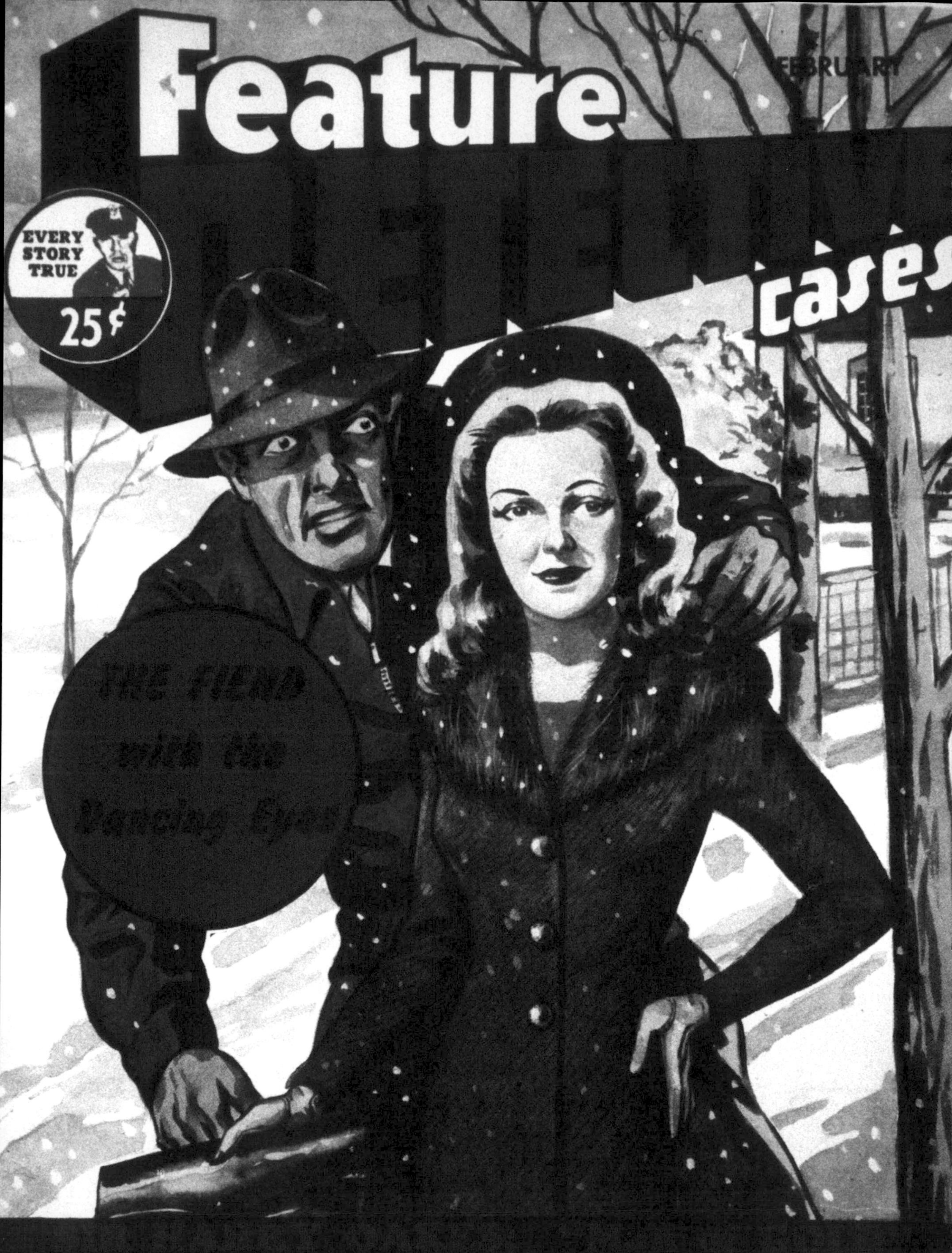
Feature
FEBRUARY
EVERY STORY TRUE
25¢
cases

such as these rarely appeared in true crime pulp stories of the 1940s. Canadian magazine publishers favoured stories that recounted how ordinary folk — car mechanics and lunch counter waitresses — who aspired to lives of luxury inevitably ended up behind bars or strung up on a scaffold. These were the kinds of people who refused to accept their station in life, to line up for an honest job or to stick it out with a boring husband. True crime stories took readers along for the ride: last stop, justice.

JUDGING MAGAZINES BY THEIR COVERS

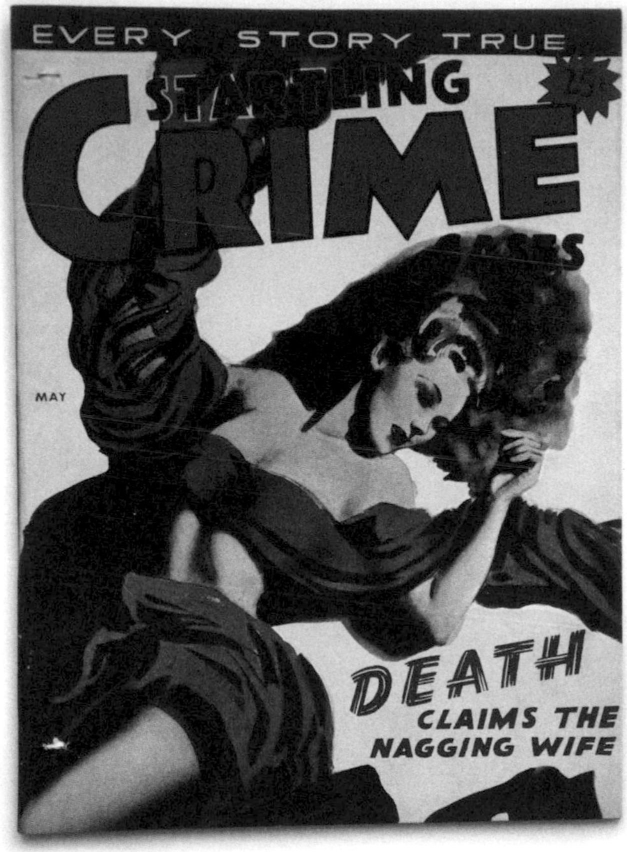
EVERY STORY TRUE
STARTLING
CRIME
CASES
MAY
DEATH
CLAIMS THE
NAGGING WIFE

No one glancing at true crime magazine covers would have guessed the conservative messages tucked within. This is one of the key features of true crime — its mixture of sexiness and moralism. The images adorning true crime magazine covers pushed the boundaries of wartime sexual propriety, while the stories were narratives of law and order. As suggestive as servicemen's pin-ups, the covers went further by combining sex with lethal violence — shootings, stabbings and strangulations. Printed in bright reds, yellows and blues, contrasted by deep shadows and swatches of black, these images still turn our heads today. Titles in chunky solid capital letters left just enough room for well-endowed women and menacing men to jump seemingly off the page. The top pulp artists, such as Norman Saunders and Rafael de Soto, worked for U.S. magazines, so Canadian publishers had to make do with cheaper local talent such as Harold Bennet and Joe Globe. Men like these were good enough to provide knock-offs of American pulp covers and Hollywood movie posters. When artists were scarce, coloured photos sufficed. Even so, Canadian pulp magazine covers were far spicier than the stories. They were meant to sell true crime and they did, in the tens of thousands every month.

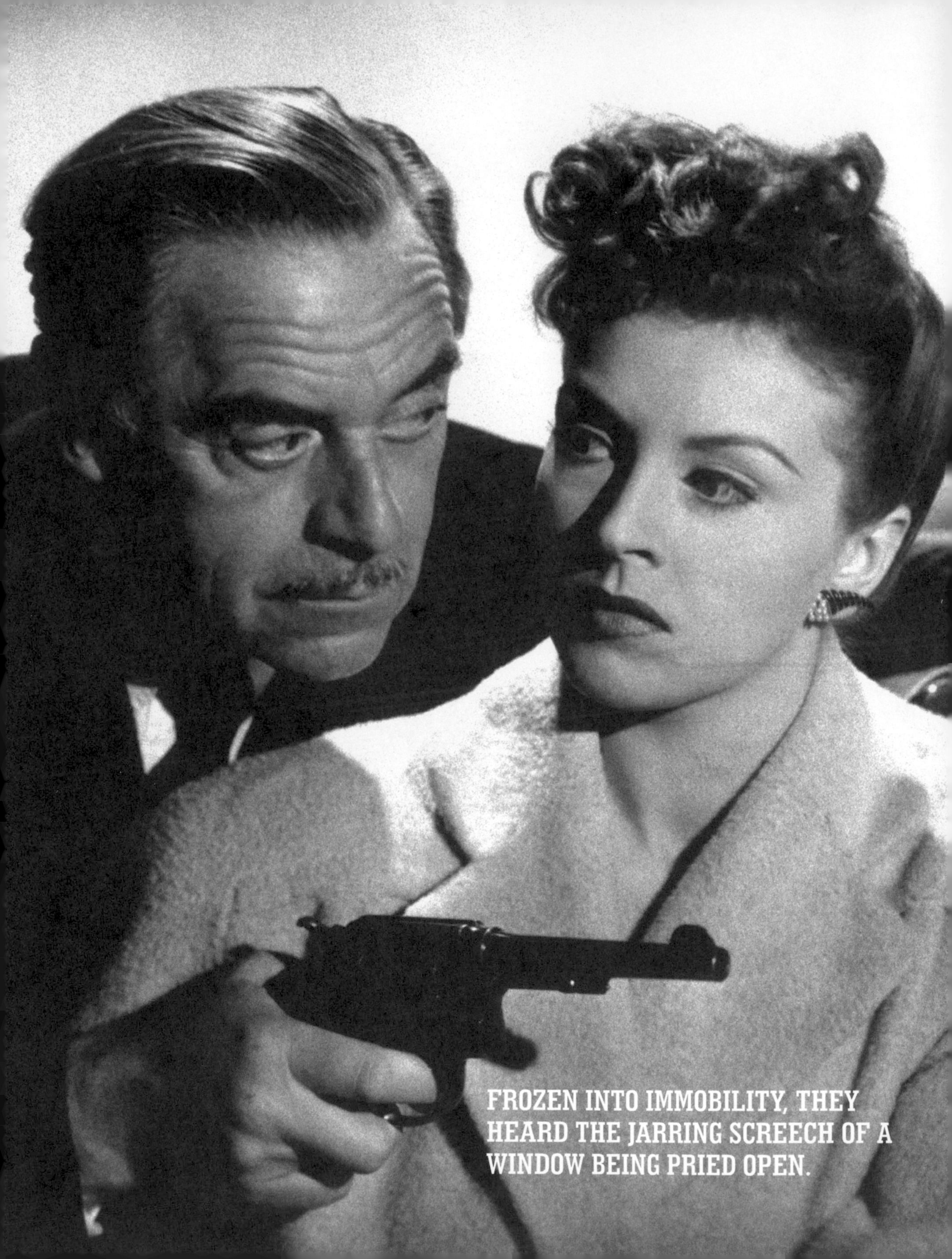

FROZEN INTO IMMOBILITY, THEY HEARD THE JARRING SCREECH OF A WINDOW BEING PRIED OPEN.

The stock figures on the covers of Canadian true crime pulps were white women, barely dressed and looking for trouble. Or scantily clad and imperilled. Or respectably dressed and in danger. Whether brunettes, blondes or redheads, these cartoonishly glamorous women invariably had long and luxurious tresses. Men were depicted with fewer adornments. Unlike crime comics and adventure stories, which often pictured bare-chested he-men, true crime cover men were fully clothed, appearing either as dangerous figures (choking or knifing women, or dragging them off) or as victims of gun-toting or blade-wielding women. While the stories traced the plodding work of professional crime fighters, the magazine covers screamed sexually charged mayhem.

Even a myopic shopper at a drugstore magazine stand could hardly fail to miss the drama jammed into a true crime cover. A step or two closer and she could make out the slogans (such as "hard-boiled but soft") that teased readers along with story titles. Canadian stories were rarely mentioned on covers but the occasional subtitle, like "Trailing Toronto's Love Slayer" or "Snaring Winnipeg's Horse-Faced Bandit," lent local flavour to the recognizably American art form. Like pulp fiction magazines, they were eye-popping on the outside but they packaged a different product: the truth, not only about crime but of crimes committed where readers lived.

Compared to the covers, the interiors of true crime magazines were far from eye-catching. While publishers expected authors to come up with crime scene and crook-catching images for their stories, authors couldn't expect to see high production values in the finished product. It took good storytelling to lift a case above the amateurish graphics and blurry pictures borrowed or bought from police contacts and newspaper offices.

ADDING TO THE THRILL

Magazine covers were the most obvious means through which design lent sexiness to sober texts. Even more significant were the advertisements that appeared inside the Canadian pulps. Ads offered readers an endless array of consumer products, many of which were hard to come by in shops. Some items, such as birth control manuals, were officially illegal in 1940s Canada, but readers could easily purchase them through magazine distribution houses. Books on contraception and marital problems could be ordered for two or three dollars and delivered discreetly "to persons over the age of 21." Printed between stories, running along sidebars and stuffed at the back of true crime magazines, ads for how-to and self-help manuals courted the attention of the

LETTER TO THE EDITOR

"Dear Editor — I find fault with your illustrations. They were skimpy and badly drawn. Either you need better artists or the artists you are using should try to improve their work ..." As this cover suggests, Edouard Maurice of Montreal had a point. Too bad the story it illustrated wasn't called "The Case of the Wall-Eyed Whipping Women."

DARING
CRIME
15¢
CASES
STRANGE STORY OF VANCOUVER CULT
TRAPPING WINNIPEG'S POCK-MARKED FRANKENSTEIN

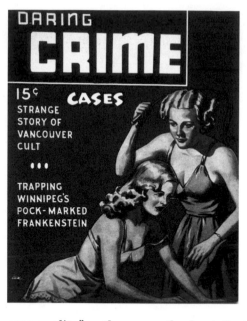

lovelorn and lusty. If reading stories of deadly love triangles and double-crossed lovers showed how love could go terribly wrong, the ads in true crime pulps reassured readers that they could avoid troubles and have a bit of fun for only a few dollars.

Advertisements were sexually provocative but they were far from sexually liberating. Here, again, the pulps betrayed their mixture of titillation and conservatism. For instance, women were advised to purchase manuals on "how to meet men and marry" and told that "prewar quality" cutlery was the best that money could buy. Men were tempted with bachelors' joke books and stories for "stags." The adventurous could opt for unblushing tales of exotic sexual practices among Eastern heathens and the anthropologically minded could select clinically pitched studies of sexual "deviants." Even timid readers, who couldn't imagine the postman delivering a book wrapped in brown paper wrapping, could get a tasty sample just by reading the ads.

FROM COVER TO COVER

The true crime pulp magazine industry that sprang up in Canada in the 1940s began to shrivel a decade later. By the 1950s Canadian pulps struggled for survival, because the lifting of wartime import restrictions meant that American magazines — glossier, flashier — made Canadian magazines, with their cheap production values and local stories, look dowdy and parochial. More significantly a new publishing format, the paperback, began to dominate the popular fiction and true crime markets, not only in Canada but the U.S., as well. Consequently, Canadian magazines such as *Famous Crime Cases* lost their competitive edge. Canadian pulp producers began to specialize in comic books, continued to produce local scandal sheets or, like Al Valentine, moved out of the publishing business altogether.

Canadian true crime magazines of the 1940s might easily have been forgotten. In a way they were meant to be: they were cheap to buy and even

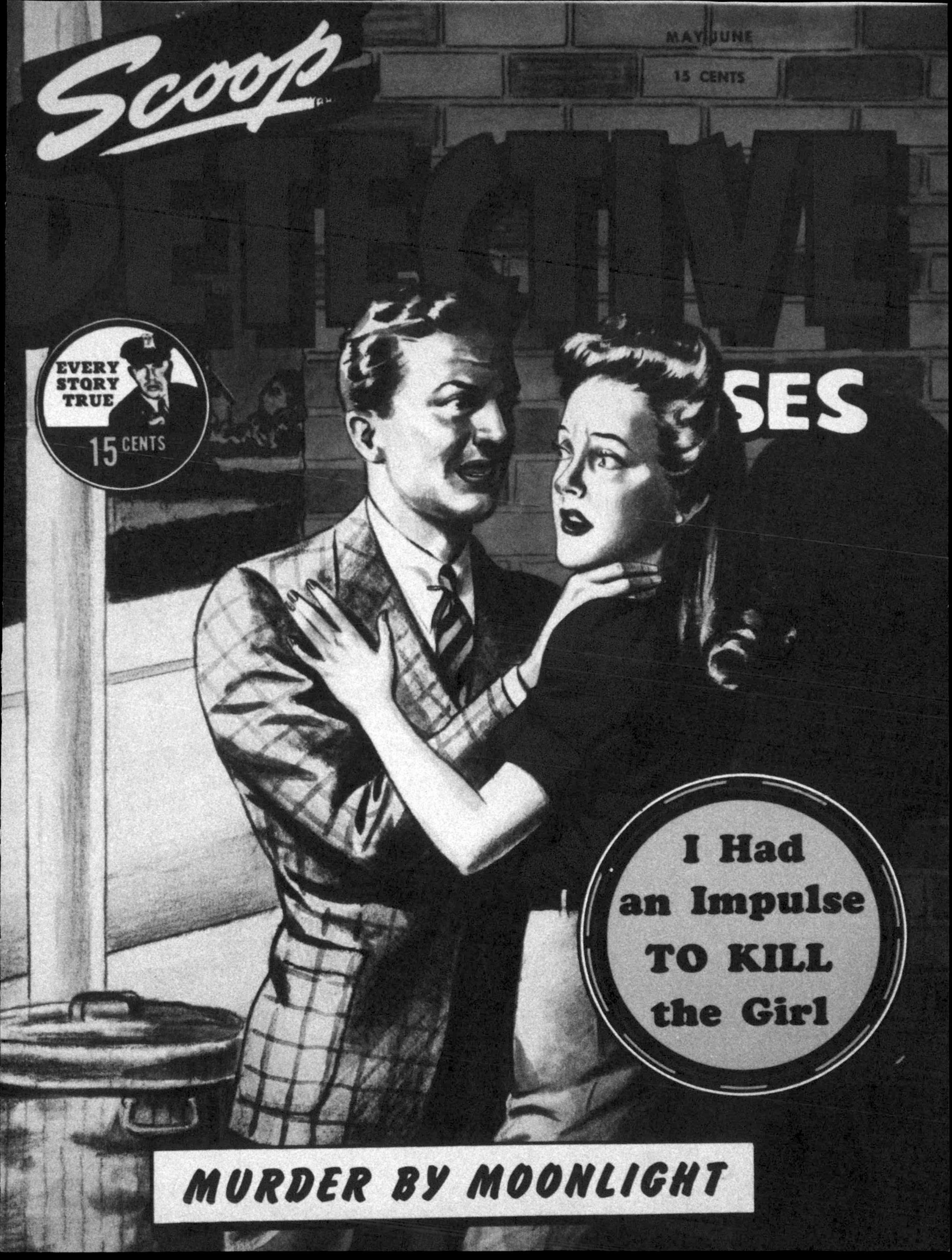
Scoop
MAY-JUNE
15 CENTS
SES
EVERY STORY TRUE
15 CENTS
I Had an Impulse TO KILL the Girl
MURDER BY MOONLIGHT

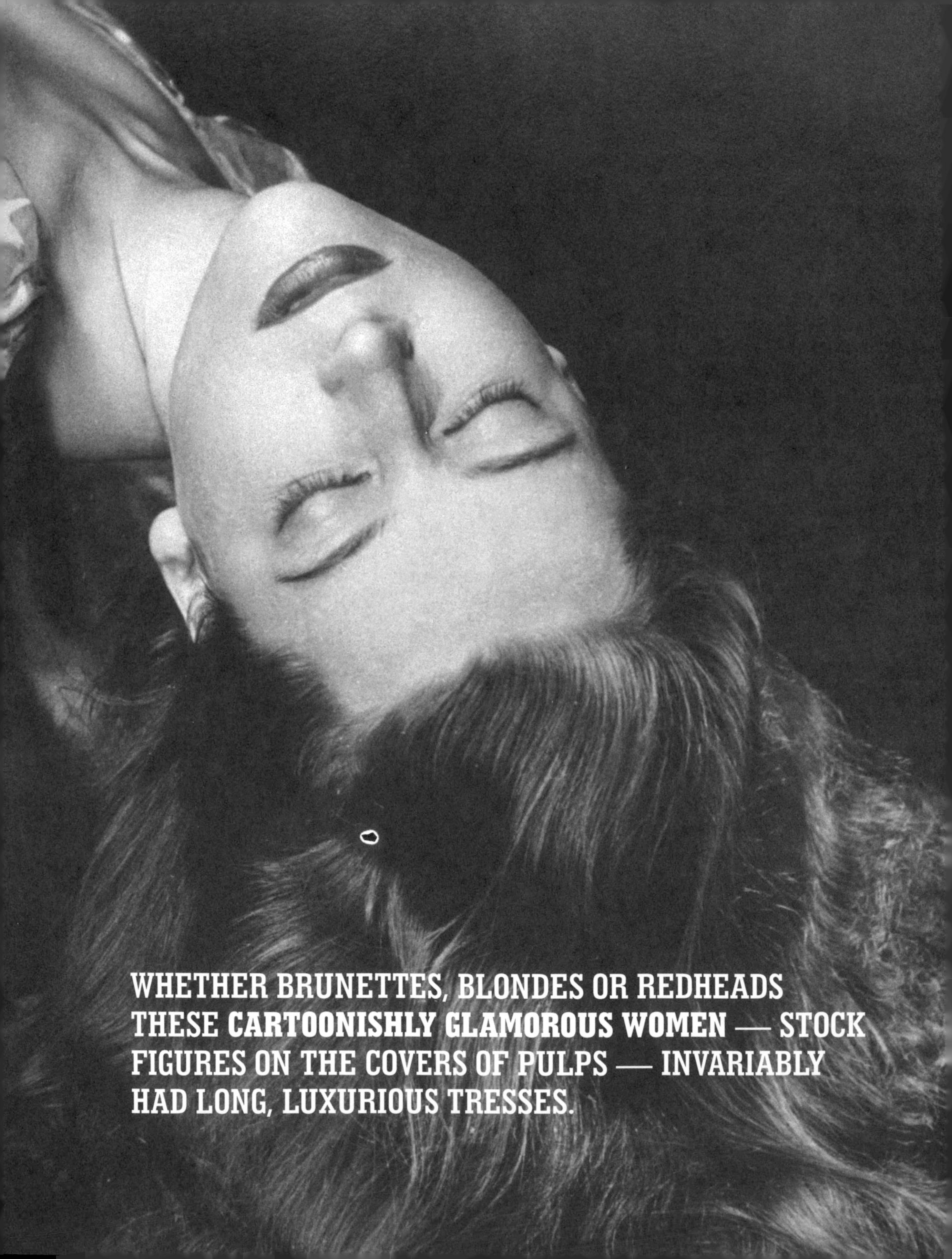

WHETHER BRUNETTES, BLONDES OR REDHEADS THESE **CARTOONISHLY GLAMOROUS WOMEN** — STOCK FIGURES ON THE COVERS OF PULPS — INVARIABLY HAD LONG, LUXURIOUS TRESSES.

more cheaply produced, made to toss away. Fortunately, ephemera and book collectors such as George Flie and Nelson Ball had a soft spot for Canadian pulps and thought they were worth preserving. A 10-cent magazine can now easily fetch $30 on the collectors' circuit. The National Library of Canada also became a pulp collector when it made a major purchase from George Flie's collection. Once meant to be consumed like movie popcorn, the pulps have recently become objects of serious scholarly inquiry — for example, communications scholar Will Straw has analyzed works in his own collection and published his findings on McGill University's Culture of Cities Project website. Only a few issues of magazines such as *Daring Crime Cases* and *Factual Detective* remain, but they can lead us back to a period when Canadians produced and purchased pulps that combined sermonizing with salaciousness, and gave true crime a distinctly Canadian flavour.

In the pages that follow we return to the pulps, affectionately and critically exploring the themes that characterized true crime in the True North: the unquestioned adherence to retributive justice, the unwavering faith in lawmen and the enduring affection for the men of the mounted. We also trace writers' preoccupation with jealousy and betrayal, the deadly consequences of greediness and the growing menace of sexual "fiends." But no journey through the pulps would be complete without ogling some flashy covers and comical ads along the way.

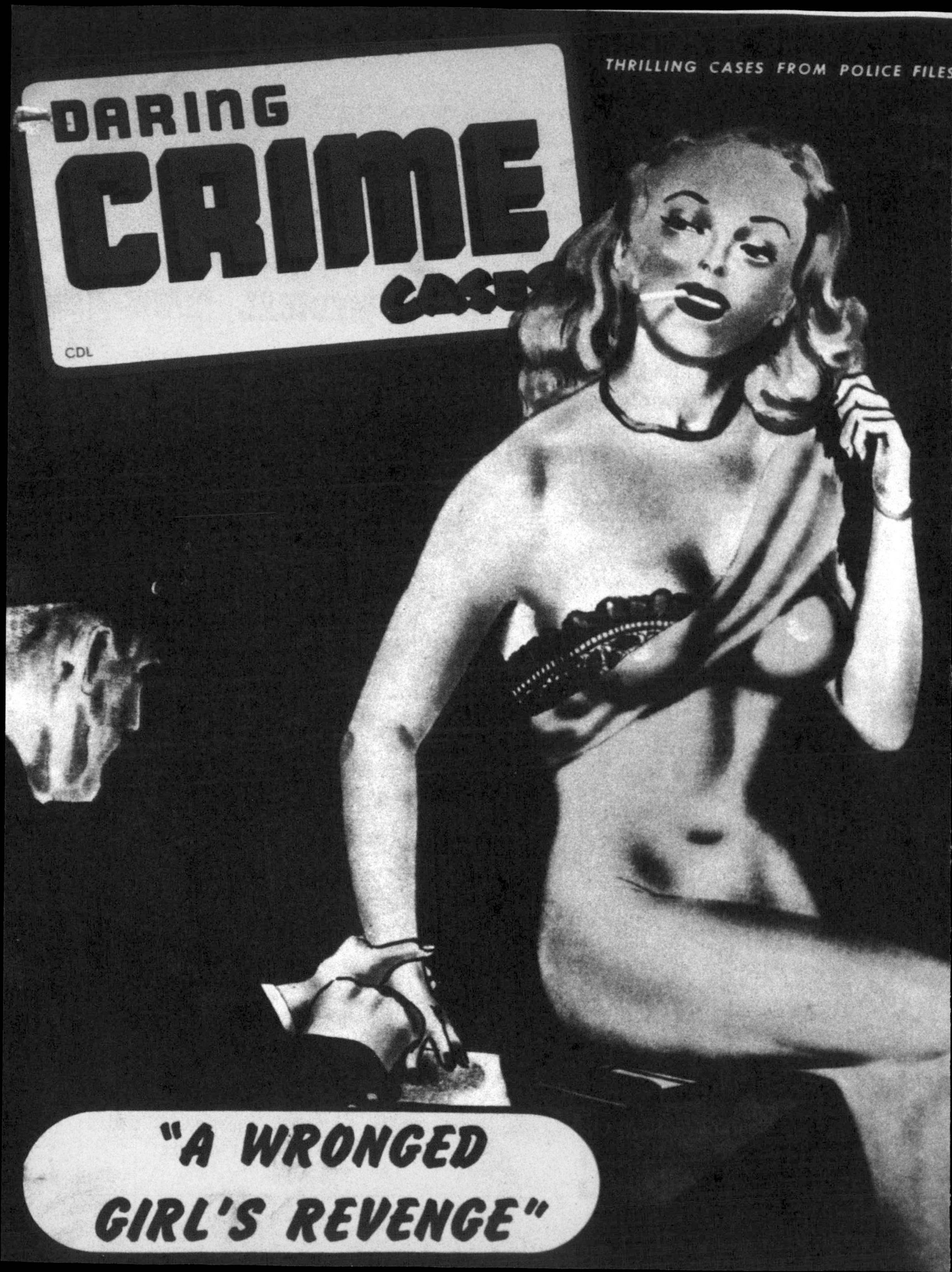
THRILLING CASES FROM POLICE FILES
DARING
CRIME
CDL
"A WRONGED
GIRL'S REVENGE"

1

VENGEANCE IS MINE, SAYETH THE LAW

ALTHOUGH COP-KILLINGS were infrequent events in Canada, they were surefire material for writers to peddle to true crime publishers. Normally the heroes in any true crime story, police officers as victims were especially tragic figures. And, of course, solving such crimes required the skills and dedication of brother officers, upholding both the law and their loyalty to their fallen comrades. In the hands of a skilful true crime writer such cases were fashioned into potent cautionary tales about the risks and costs of crime.

While messages like these were standard true crime features in the 1940s pulps, stories about cop-killings conveyed two particular moral messages: namely, that killers of officers would always, no matter how crafty or ruthless, be tracked down and punished, and that the police alone were justified in using deadly force. State vengeance, in the form of imprisonment and execution, was morally and legally distinct from criminal revenge, according to the pulps — the only legitimate avenging angels were those who were cloaked in uniforms, bearing the authority of the state.

Kept within bounds, however, the urge to fight back or stick up for oneself did not constitute a criminal act. Pulp ads for bodybuilding techniques and boxing lessons aimed to convince readers that forcefulness was a key ingredient in manliness. Playing on stereotypes that linked masculinity to brute strength and pugilistic skills, one such ad asked: "In an emergency would your actions show the lady in your life you are a MAN?" Doubts could be dispelled by mailing in the coupon for *Jack Dempsey's American Combat*

Judo, which promised to buttress the buyer's manhood in "55 quick and easy lessons."

Stories and ads like these relied on and reinforced existing gender stereotypes, but they stopped short of encouraging readers to take the law into their own hands. As the cover featuring a "Wronged Girl's Revenge" suggested, jilted lovers and cheated rivals had no right to commit murder even if their motives were understandable. The law's violence was of a finer quality — judicious, measured and a necessary element of civil society. Canada's finest didn't settle scores, seek retribution or engage in reprisals. Any violence inflicted by law officers or Canada's hangman was justice in action.

THE ANATOMY OF A MURDER

In Canada's true crime magazines there were three ways to kill a cop or turnkey: in a shootout trying to avoid capture, in a jailbreak trying to avoid punishment or out of revenge. Although the circumstances surrounding such murders differed, as did the lessons to be derived from them, stories about cop-killings underscored their singular brutality, the bestiality of the killers and the humanity of their victims.

For instance, when Winnipeg safecracker Mike Atamonchuk and his henchmen found themselves surrounded by city police during one of their heists, they shot their way to freedom in "a smoking inferno of flashing guns, splintering glass and muffled curses." When quiet returned, Officer John Macdonald lay dead and his partner wounded. Faced with the grim duty of informing a young wife and mother that her husband had fallen in the line of duty, Chief George Smith trudged back to the station to begin the hunt for "Winnipeg's Horse-Faced Bandit." According to writer Philip Godsell, Smith was spurred on by the plaintive cries of the Macdonalds' six-year-old: "'Daddy won't be here anymore!'"

Wanted for trespassing on traplines near Fort McPherson, in the Northwest Territories, Albert Johnson's bid to stay out of jail was even more spectacular. "The Mad Trapper of Rat River" holed himself up in a log fortress before fleeing deeper into the wilderness, defying the "warrants, guns and dynamite bombs of the Mounties" for many weeks. A skilled marksman, the trapper managed to wound one constable and kill another before being filled with lead himself on February 17, 1932, taking the secret of his origins and his motives with him.

Despite the dramatic circumstances that led to these homicides, pulp writers resisted any inclination to romanticize the criminals, portraying them as men who killed only to defend themselves or as eccentric loners. In Godsell's view, cop-killers were vicious animals who didn't hesitate to turn on their own when cornered. When one of "Mike the Horse's" henchmen took the wounded robber to his girlfriend's house for safekeeping, Atamonchuk apparently expressed his gratitude by threatening to kill them if he were caught.

It might have been possible to see trapper Albert Johnson as a victim of the police, a single man hounded by nine Mounties, 42 dogs and one airplane. But Philip Godsell didn't, and he referred to his interview with the RCMP pilot involved in the chase to underscore the fact the "Mad Trapper" got his just desserts. Johnson died "'with the most awful grimace of hate….'" One look at that and, the pilot confessed, he "'couldn't feel sorry'" for him. "'Instead,'" he continued, "'I was glad he was dead. The world seemed a cleaner place without him.'"

If there was a moral to these stories of the brief and violent lives of cop-killers like Mike Atamonchuk and Albert Johnson, it was that this sort of crime "paid only one dividend: the dividend of death!" Had both men merely surrendered, both their lives and those of their victims would have been spared. By killing their pursuers they signed their own death warrants. While the trapper died with his mukluks on, in a shootout, "'Mike the Horse' cheated the gallows" by committing suicide, fittingly "with the very gun that had claimed his victim." He also framed his partners in crime, leaving them to serve 20 years each in Manitoba's Stony Mountain Penitentiary, where, as Godsell smugly concluded, they would have "ample time to meditate on that ancient adage: Crime does not pay."

PUBLIC ENEMIES

While criminals who killed lawmen often did so in the course of committing other crimes, there were others, such as Jean McMinn and her pals, who resorted to violence to break out of jail. Dubbed "Canada's Female Public Enemy No. 1" by writer John Russell, 16-year-old McMinn was, "in the parlance of the underworld … a tough baby." On one hand, she was born bad: "In her blood," Russell wrote, "was the irrepressible craving for adventure." But Russell mixed this "bad seed" interpretation of Jean's waywardness with a little pop psychology: "Her home life was almost nil, her parents having been divorced when she was seven years old." Without proper parental guidance, she began to "display anti-social symptoms and develop into a major problem for the aunt and uncle with whom she lived in Toronto's east end." Her life was a "continual round of movies by day and petting parties by night," and culminated — predictably — in her incarceration for "incorrigibility" in 1925. With "no colourful boyfriends ... [and] no petting" to distract her at the Women's Jail Farm, McMinn entertained herself by plotting an escape that

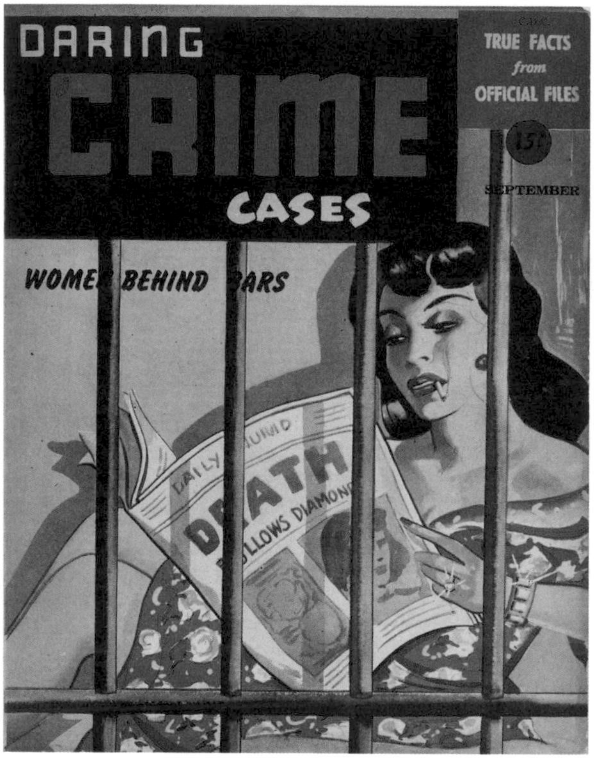
DARING
CRIME
CASES
TRUE FACTS
from
OFFICIAL FILES
15¢
SEPTEMBER
WOME BEHIND ARS

HER LIFE WAS A "CONTINUAL ROUND OF MOVIES BY DAY AND PETTING PARTIES BY NIGHT," AND CULMINATED — PREDICTABLY — IN HER INCARCERATION FOR "INCORRIGIBILITY" IN 1925.

left 200-pound prison matron Margaret Mick dead. Jean and her two friends were wanted women.

The exploits of McMinn and her companions were repeated almost 20 years later by a group of three boys, inmates of Winnipeg's Vaughan Street Detention Home. Leslie Young, aged 17, Lewis McNeill, 14, and George Janssens, 15, were "juvenile delinquents" incarcerated for minor offences in 1943. Young and McNeill were repeat offenders, facing a total of seven criminal charges, while Janssens was experiencing his first visit to Vaughan, for stealing a bicycle. Despite their tender years, they apparently plotted their escape with a "cold and merciless deliberation ... worthy of hardened and astute criminals."

Staging a disturbance to lure guard Edwin Pearse into their dormitory, the three boys pounced on the 58-year-old "like a tornado ... of whirling arms and striking fists," stole his keys and escaped into a snowy Remembrance Day night. Soon afterward, Vaughan Street's other staff discovered the body of their comrade, shocked that a "hale and hearty" man could be "struck lifeless by three young thugs whose joint ages aggregated less than his own."

Both "Canada's Female Public Enemy No. 1," Russell's story of a trio of female jailbreakers, and "Death Stalks the Night," Godsell's chronicle of Edwin Pearse's murder at the hands of three wartime juvenile delinquents, appeared at a time when there was great anxiety about the economic and social disruptions of the Second World War. The conflict had thrust men into battle and women into factory overalls, leaving youth unsupervised and prone to moral ruin. In the opinion of many of the country's social critics, Canada stood to lose the war at home if parents didn't maintain over their children the same discipline as its soldiers exhibited on the battlefield.

In this context these two stories, published in 1943 and 1944, served as cautionary wartime tales. Russell delivered his message by detailing Jean McMinn's tumultuous family history and allowing his readers to make the connection between her broken home and life of crime. Godsell, on the other hand, took a much more direct approach, invoking guard Pearse's belief that juvenile delinquency was attributable to parents "who denied the youngsters the home training and attention needed to mould them into law-abiding and decent citizens." Godsell ended his story with a public service announcement: "To parents engaged in war work and unable to keep an eye on wayward offspring," he wrote, "the case of these three youngsters ... should prove a pointed and salutary warning."

COLD-HEARTED KILLERS

If ever there was a Canadian crime tailor-made for a true crime pulp, it was the murder of a British Columbia Provincial Police constable in 1921. Still inspirational today (its latest rendition has appeared in the form of an opera, *Filumena*), the crime provided fodder for several writers who sold their versions to Canadian pulps in the 1940s. In each of these accounts, the location of the killing, Alberta's Crowsnest Pass, was the place where the Wild West met the Jazz Age, with tragic consequences.

The brutal slaying of Constable Steve Lawson confirmed the all-too-common violence that had plagued the provincial border zone since it had been taken over by a gang of Italian bootleggers. In Philip Godsell's version it went like this: in the shade of the saw-toothed mountains, crime boss Emilio "Emperor Pic" Picariello had amassed a fortune running illegal shipments of booze between Alberta and British Columbia. When Constable Lawson shot and wounded the bootlegger's son after a wild car chase, the "Emperor" and his consort, Florence Lassandro, planned their revenge, driving to Lawson's house and shooting the constable in front of his horrified wife and children.

Unlike killings during jailbreaks or shootouts with police in pursuit, deliberate acts of revenge against lawmen were premeditated and therefore wholly inexcusable. C. V. Tench (writing as "Ned Ward") wrote a version of the case, centred on two contrasting images: Picariello and Lassandro plotting revenge with their conniving crime family; and off-duty Constable Lawson, unaware of what was about to transpire, lounging "in slippered ease," surrounded by his five children. Nine-year-old Pearl testified tearfully in court: "That's the lady who shot my daddy!"

For Philip Godsell, the Alikomiak case was equally odious because it involved an Inuit man who had betrayed the trust and kindness of his supposed civilizers, the men in scarlet. Alikomiak came to the Mounties' attention after he and an accomplice, Tatamagana killed a man whose wife Alikomiak desired. Arrested and charged with the murder, he spent his days awaiting trial in Fort McPherson, Northwest Territories, under the kindly watch of "round-faced and beaming" Bill Doak of the mounted. With no holding cell or shackles available, Corporal Doak gave his prisoner the run of the settlement, putting him to work at odd jobs and allowing him to sleep in the Mountie barracks at night. The "slim, sloe-eyed youth" did everything he was asked "with a smile," but secretly seethed with resentment. When Doak chastised the young man for not properly chewing the corporal's sealskin boots — "a duty usually assigned by the natives to their wives" — Alikomiak plotted his revenge.

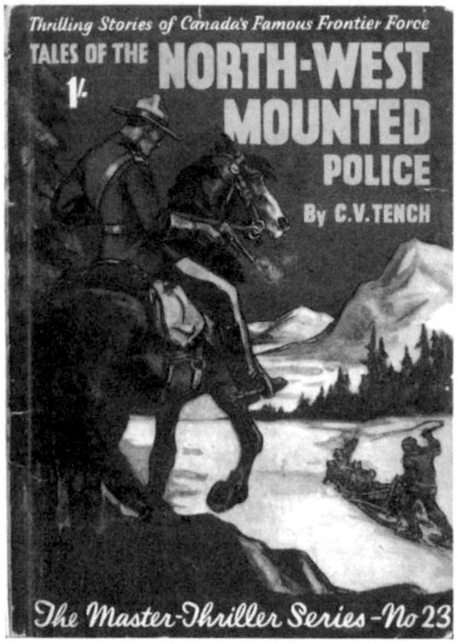
Thrilling Stories of Canada's Famous Frontier Force
TALES OF THE NORTH-WEST MOUNTED POLICE
1/-
By C.V. TENCH
The Master-Thriller Series - No 23

Some true crime magazine authors like North Vancouver's C. V. Tench cut their teeth writing dime novels or collections of short stories about "Canada's Famous Frontier Force." This one was produced for an English audience by London's Work's World in 1938. (Glenbow Library, Calgary Alberta)

Rather than simply walk away from Fort McPherson, he used the freedom he had been afforded to steal a rifle and cartridges. Instead of killing the sleeping officer, he decided "he would shoot Doak in the leg and wound him … want[ing] him to suffer, but not, apparently, to die." According to Godsell, "the policeman … lived for about four hours, paralysed, and had asked him [Alikomiak] why he'd done this thing." The "Smiling Killer" had no answer.

Alikomiak's disingenuous smile was the obvious marker of his cunning criminality. According to Godsell, the Inuit of the western Arctic were a "motley horde of Mongol-faced humanity," some of whom would "cut your throat for a box of cartridges." This convention of connecting appearance and behaviour was typical of true crime writing, including those dealing with nonaboriginals. For example, Albert Johnson was a human "wolverine," with teeth that "glistened like animal fangs through his thick bristle beard," betraying his subhuman qualities. Mike Atamonchuk was "horse-faced," and Emilio Picariello a "gorilla."

"Long lashed and lovely" Florence Lassandro was no hirsute knuckle-scraper, but thanks to the active imagination of Philip Godsell her criminal tendencies were manifested in a love of finery and, like Alikomiak, an inappropriate nonchalance that slid into cruelty. Her scarlet tam, brilliant green coat and high heels allowed police to place her at the crime scene, but it was her defiance that first cast her in a suspicious light. Greeting the officers at her door with an "impudent smile," Lassandro rejected their reassurances about the questioning that would follow, in Godsell's rendition of the exchange:

"IT'S ABOUT THE KILLING OF CONSTABLE LAWSON," [SERGEANT] SCOTT TOLD HER. "BUT YOU NEEDN'T BE AFRAID."

"HE'S DEAD AND I'M ALIVE," SHE [LASSANDRO] LAUGHED LIGHTLY. "I'VE NOTHING TO BE AFRAID OF."

Even after her indictment Lassandro continued to defy decorum, blowing kisses to friends in the courtroom and telling them, "'Don't worry, I'll be with you soon.'"

The link between appearance and behaviour in true crime stories drew on everything from fairy tales to 19th-century criminology, and wasn't limited to the pulps. In the funny pages, square-jawed and clean-cut Dick Tracy matched wits with the likes of "Flattop," "Mole," "Pear-Shape" and "Prune Face," characters that paralleled true crime villains like "Winnipeg's Pock-Marked Frankenstein," "The Man with the Big Ears," "The Killer Who Never Smiled" and "The Wall-Eyed Gunman."

Canada's Mounties didn't sport Dick Tracy's jaunty fedora and sharp trench coat, but for the adoring women who peopled the pages of the country's pulps there was nothing like an Anglo-Canadian man in a uniform. As one fan admitted, "that nice red coat goes to my head like champagne!" The effervescent charms of the force only made their deaths in the line of duty all the more tragic. Not only were those felled by criminals exemplary officers, but they were also exemplary people: handsome, brave Anglo-Canadian men, who left behind young families and grieving communities.

Steve Lawson, "the genial 34-year-old officer, whose honesty and fairness

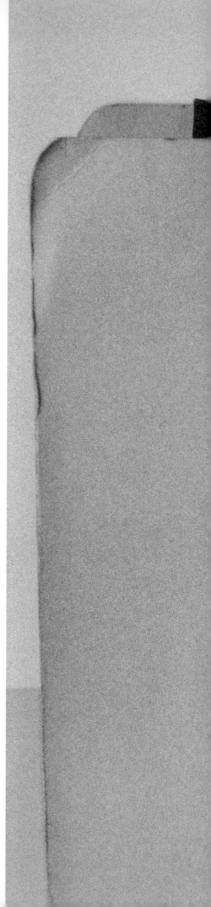

were a byword in the Pass," had also "distinguished himself on the fields of France" in the First World War. He was, in Godsell's account, a loving husband to "trim humorous-eyed … Mrs. Lawson" and a doting father to his five children, including Pearl, who loved to play with his loaded revolver (!).

Winnipeg's Constable John Macdonald, one of Mike the Horse's victims, also left behind a young child, "who seemed to realize that his six-foot daddy, the strongest and kindest man he knew, would never gather him in his arms again."

Matron Margaret Mick, the guard slain by the jazz babies, was a career corrections officer "loved by thousands of troubled girls during her thirty years' service." According to her son-in-law, "every person who knew her spoke very highly of her character. If she could not say anything good about a prisoner to the authorities above her she would not say anything at all."

Similarly, guard Edwin Pearse was remembered by his neighbours as a hard-working man who "had a cheery word for everyone who passed" his neatly kept house. The war veteran "always had a warm spot in his heart" for the "young unfortunates" he kept watch over, until three punks cruelly ended his life.

AVENGING ANGELS

Deaths of deserving people like these justified the full force of the law, but true crime writers were careful not to call it "revenge." That was for criminals. What the police sought was "vengeance," a word that had religious connotations and linked the lawmen's actions to that of a wrathful God. The police went after cop-killers like "grim avenging spirits" or "flinty-eyed avenging demons," delivering "hammer blows" against all those who

SPECIALLY POSED PICTURES
Publishers might have prided themselves on stories based on "true facts from official files," but they didn't have any problem with using "specially posed" pictures to illustrate stories. Just in case his photographer lacked inspiration, Al Valentine kept a file of movie stills and "cheesecake photos" so his subjects could mimic the appropriate horrified, evil or seductive poses. More often than not, what started as cheesecake ended up as simply cheesy.

24

NA

ILLUSTRATIONS:

Pin-Up and Spicy

CHEESECAKE
PHOTOS

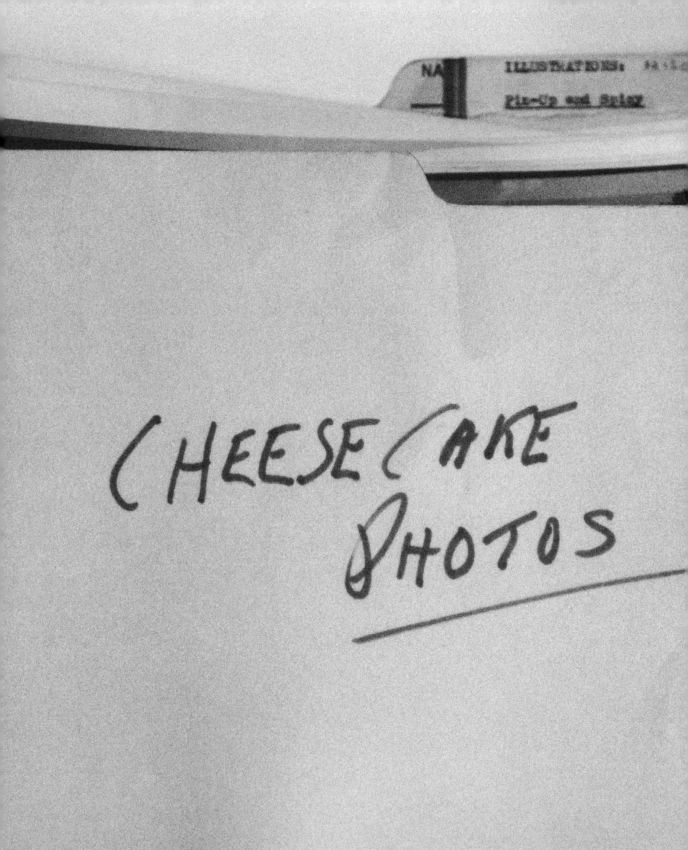

tried to stop them. But that didn't mean they acted precipitously, or out of personal grudges.

If revenge was a dish best served cold, then the righteous vengeance prepared by the police came straight out of the freezer. In the pulps, state vengeance was carefully plotted, its execution methodical. Following Lawson's death, for instance, the B.C. Provincial Police launched a coordinated assault on the "dives, joints and gambling halls" that Emperor Pic supplied, as well as his own store of moonshine. "In the depths of the purple-shadowed valleys," Godsell wrote, the Mounties had "smelled out hidden liquor caves, spilled the whiskey on the moss" and arrested Pic's son. At the same time, they "gathered evidence with which to build up a cast-iron case" against the king and queen of the Crowsnest Pass, carefully going over the forensic evidence, "tracing angles of trajectory," comparing ballistics reports and reinterviewing witnesses.

The investigation into Mountie Bill Doak's murder was equally systematic and disciplined — despite the temptation to go after the killer with guns a-blazing. After Constable Woolams had wrestled Alikomiak into submission and slapped on the cuffs, he was approached by an Inuit chief. Offering the constable an axe, the chief suggested "'mebbe better kill'um right now so he [Alikomiak] no make it more trouble.'" Here was a chance for the Mountie to take revenge — but Woolams didn't take the "savage" option. As Godsell wrote, "it was with disgust and wonder at the white man's strange ways that the Cogmollocks [Copper Inuit] saw Aligoomiak [sic] taken away from the village alive" to face trial.

Whereas the premeditated quality of the revenge murders committed by Pic, Lassandro and Alikomiak singled them out as particularly cold-blooded cop-killers, true crime writers framed the same calculation and planning undertaken by the police as an example of their judicious professionalism. Wreaked in the name of the law, police vengeance upheld order and civilization. Without their efforts, the Crowsnest Pass would be "a den of iniquity," where "respectable women dare not leave their homes at night." Similar sentiments accompanied the end of the Alikomiak story, but for Godsell there was an additional benefit to be reaped from the hanging. Not only had Doak been "avenged," but the western Arctic had also "been made safe at last for pioneering whites." In the North, vengeance delivered at the hands of Mounties was also a tool of colonization and an assertion of Canadian sovereignty.

What set police vengeance apart from the revenge wrought by the bad guys was not just the quality of the victims or the larger purposes it served. The virtue of police vengeance was that it was rational, rule-bound and fair. Compared with the emotional, arbitrary whims and uncontrolled passions of

FREE NEWSPAPER INSTITUTE OF AMERICA
One Park Avenue, New York 16, N.Y., U.S.A.

Send me, without cost or obligation, your Writing Aptitude Test and further information about writing for profit.

Miss
Mrs.
Mr. ______________________

Address ______________________

(All correspondence confidential. No salesman will call on you)

90-L-665

the criminal, the rule of law stood as tall and proud as the manly officer of the mounted.

So superior was principled vengeance that it could be tempered by mercy and still be just. The state could exact an eye for an eye, but Canadian justice also acknowledged the unique circumstances of individual crimes and criminals. The young offenders who killed Margaret Mick and Edwin Pearse were not convicted of murder, largely because they were underage and products of dubious parenting. Instead, jurors found them guilty of manslaughter and determined that the guard's death was accidental. Jean McMinn got five years in the Women's Prison at Kingston, while Leslie Young and Lewis McNeill were sent away for 23 months and 18 months. George Janssens, the young bicycle thief, was even more fortunate: he was found not guilty.

In the Canadian pulps, the police brought cop-killers to justice not by meting out punishment themselves but by bringing them to trial and "letting the law take its course." Though some died in a hail of bullets, in the ideal case the state's power came from the unfolding of a bureaucratic process and not the barrel of a gun. Depersonalized and humanized in this way, vengeance was just; what was a vice in criminals was transformed into a police virtue. In Canada's true crime magazines, stories of shooting the sheriff were, oddly, opportunities to remind readers of the superiority of the law.

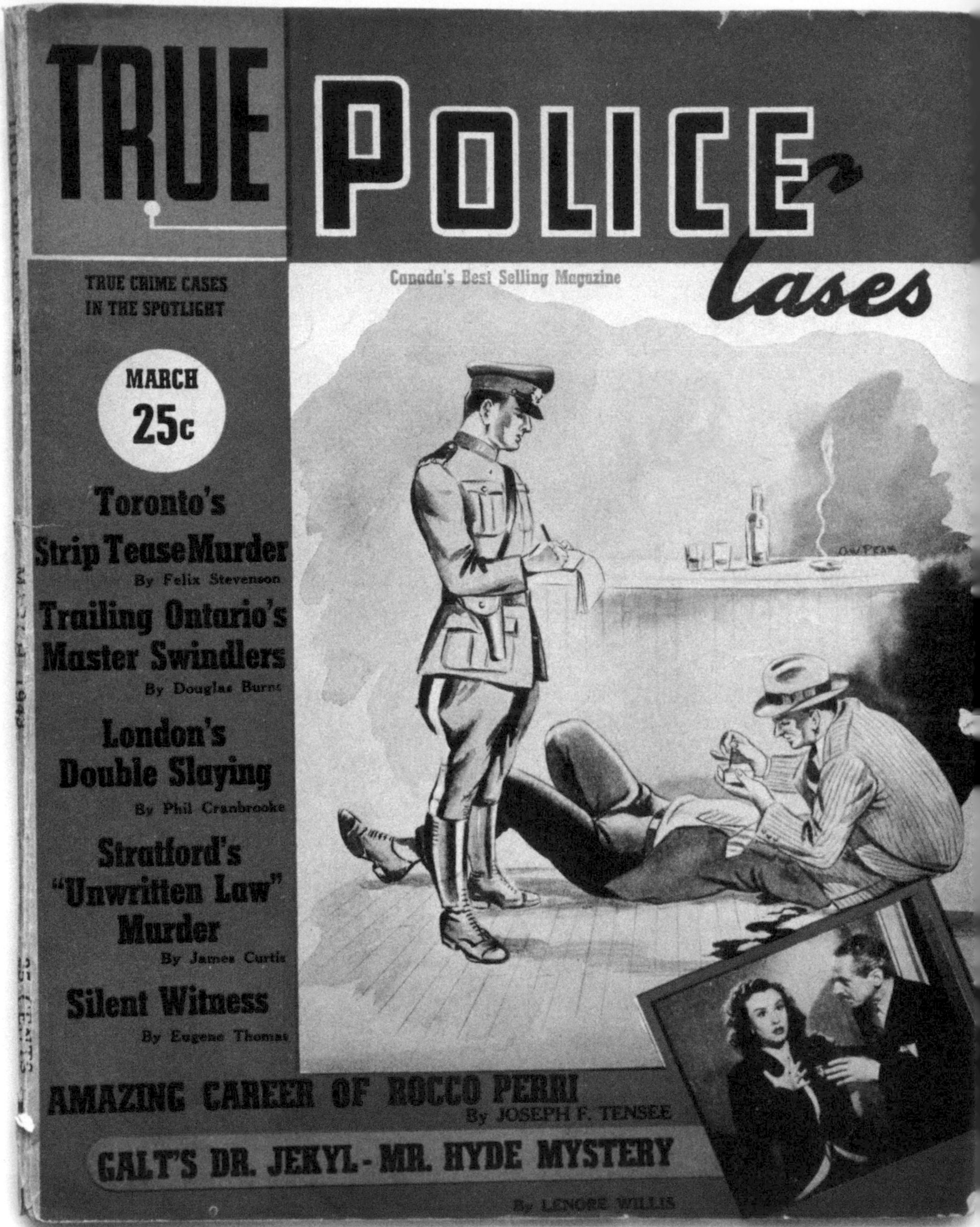
TRUE POLICE Cases
Canada's Best Selling Magazine
TRUE CRIME CASES IN THE SPOTLIGHT
MARCH
25c
Toronto's Strip Tease Murder
By Felix Stevenson
Trailing Ontario's Master Swindlers
By Douglas Burns
London's Double Slaying
By Phil Cranbrooke
Stratford's "Unwritten Law" Murder
By James Curtis
Silent Witness
By Eugene Thomas
AMAZING CAREER OF ROCCO PERRI
By JOSEPH F. TENSEE
GALT'S DR. JEKYL - MR. HYDE MYSTERY
By LENORE WILLIS

2

THEY ALWAYS GET THEIR MAN (AND SOMETIMES THEIR WOMEN, TOO)

As Craven mushed along ... he was seeing in his mind's eye a grim, relentless figure trailing along behind him. Corporal Brainard of the Mounted. The thought increased his panic, for he knew Corporal Brainard, knew him to be a tireless, relentless hunter of evildoers. The fact that he must have at least two or three days start did not ease his fears. He knew the reputation of the members of the Mounted. True, there were those who sneered at that reputation, who said it was a lot of nonsense. But Craven, like all men who knew intimately of the Mounted Police and their work, knew that it was true. The Mounted never give up . . .

— C. V. TENCH, "PANIC" (1938) IN *DARING CRIME CASES*

THE EPONYMOUS COP AND CRIMINAL in "Panic" might have been a little over the top, but C. V. Tench's tale about a homicidal trapper in Canada's Far North was nonetheless typical. Accounts like this, which celebrated the power of Canada's lawmen — mainly Mounties but some provincial police as well — made up a large portion of true crime stories published in Canada. In the True North, the forces of good and evil did battle in the frozen Arctic, on remote Prairie farms and in the twisted mountain passes of British Columbia, rarely if ever meeting in the back alleys or plush hotels of its big cities as they did in American and British stories.

The Manichean world of these Canadian true crime tales was part of another literary tradition, that of the "Northern." The plot lines and characterizations found in pulp stories like "Panic" were replicated in hundreds of dime novels, boys' and men's magazines, radio plays and B movies that circulated throughout the English-speaking world. More broadly, they were also part of a larger genre of detective and mystery writing called the "police procedural." Joe Weider, American bodybuilder and later publisher of men's magazines, couldn't get enough of them. Exhorting author Philip Godsell to "rush in" as much Canadian material as possible, he wrote: "I feel sure you can contribute good instructive and interesting articles for young men concerning Indians and Eskimos and also the Royal Canadian Mounted Police."

LETTER TO THE EDITOR

"Dear Editor — I would like to read more stories by Canadian authors referring to the Canadian scene. Now that we have magazines that are edited and published by Canadians, using Canadian paper, I believe that we should see Canadian authors in these magazines."

It almost goes without saying that, like the stories discussed in the previous chapter, these true crime Northerns also reinforced constituted authority, emphasizing as they did the supremacy of the police and their inevitable triumph over malefactors like Craven. Less apparent, however, is what true crime writers had to say about the foundations of that supremacy.

In Canadian true crime magazines, police power came from the lawmen's wits and not their brawn. The appropriately named Corporal Brainard and his comrades won their battles with the bad guys by outsmarting them, not outgunning them. Meticulous attention to detail, dogged discipline and an acute understanding of human nature cracked cases and committed criminals to the gallows. But implicit in these stories, as well, was the idea that the officers' superior intelligence reflected a more general and encompassing supremacy that stemmed from who they were individually and collectively; everything from their public appearance to their private lives worked to maintain the right.

OFFICERS AND GENTLEMEN

While brain power rather than brawn exemplified police power, there was little doubt that Canada's cops were fine specimens of Anglo-Canadian manhood. The heroes of these true crime tales were officers named Morgan, Clarke, McGill, Taylor, Russell and Alexander, many of whom had distinguished themselves on the battlefields of Europe in the Great War. By contrast, their nemeses had names like Courvoisier, Vermilyea, Koenig, Zablotny, Radko, Alikomiak and Watanabe.

Whereas criminals were as ugly as sin, true crime cops were just the opposite: six-footers to a man, they were possessed of broad shoulders, good postures and clear complexions, and sported just enough facial hair to confirm

SINFUL CITIES OF THE WESTERN WORLD

By HENDRIK DE LEEUW

This book tells of the horror and barter of human flesh in—

BERLIN — Where the Kultur tenets of Fascism and its strange degeneracies result in a variety of curious expressions.

•

PARIS—With its sordid tales of women. Here we meet Monsieur L— of the Surete and La Plage, head of the great female importing business.

•

ALGIERS—Whose Kasbah harbors the renegades of many races — veiled Algerian and Arab women, Berber girls, bright-eyed Jewish women from the Oiran and Constantine, Negro girls from the desert oasis—with young eyes grown hard in their ancient profession.

•

TANGIER—Where the strangest freaks of nature, the Maricones, cater to the Moor, and where, under the very nose of the French, brown and copper girls are shipped to the dives of the whites and white girls to the B[illegible]s.

•

SIDI-BEL-ABBES—The headquarters of the men of the Foreign Legion, to satisfy whom, a great industry thrives, cherished by the authorities.

•

MARSEILLES — The hybrid city, where Eastern evil and Western vice blend.

•

Specially Priced to Clear
Limited Stock:
Price Prepaid $2.49

ALEXANDER SALES COMPANY

95 King St., East, Suite 304
Toronto, Ontario, Canada

their masculinity, or so it seemed. Philip Godsell's Sergeant J. D. Nicholson was typical: a "loose-limbed, scarlet-coated man with the clipped military moustache," his "suntanned face and steely-grey eyes" reassured the law-abiding even as it struck fear in the hearts of evildoers.

These were patriotic, vigorous hemen who didn't smoke, drink or otherwise engage in behaviours that would interfere in the discharge of their duties or the care of their trusty steeds. Though chaste, they were not innocent of the ways of the world, and more specifically of the ways of men — and women. Underneath the scarlet uniform, Mountie blood ran fast and red.

Although the private lives of Canada's lawmen were rarely featured in any kind of detail, there was little doubt about their heterosexuality. Straighter arrows never flew than the uniformed officers in Canada's true crime magazines. True crime cops not only got their men but routinely snagged their women, as well — sometimes literally.

When rancher Isaac Belt disappeared in 1902, the North West Mounted Police wasted no effort in searching for him. After discovering his body in the Red Deer River they focused their energies on capturing his killer, arresting a young American who was wearing some of the rancher's clothes. Tried and convicted for Belt's murder, Ernest Casshel was sentenced to death in December 1903 but escaped just a few days before he was to be executed. Once again, the NWMP dispatched officers to get their man — for a second time. As C. V. Tench told it in "Casshel's Escape," the convict might not have been nabbed had his girlfriend not "transferred her affections to a young Mounted Policeman, one of the very men now searching for [him]."

Casshel's case aside, most members of Canada's police forces didn't mix business with pleasure, but that didn't mean they denied themselves the company of women. Far from it. Exercising their chivalrous charms, many of the country's finest ended up married men. They were, of course, loyal husbands with devoted wives and clutches of winsome children, a testimony to the kind of domesticated masculinity and conventionality that were the foundations of social stability.

If by virtue of their physical traits, cultural background and family status Canadian true crime cops embodied the normal, the other values they upheld — cooperation and uncompromising fairness — only served to heighten their pre-eminence. In the True North, lawmen weren't lone rangers because chasing criminals across vast uninhabited territories was a collective effort. Both federal and provincial police were quick to put egos aside and join forces with each other, as well as with their brothers-in-arms below the 49th parallel.

But solidarity in the face of crime didn't preclude a little healthy competition within the ranks, as was the case in the hunt for escaped convict Casshel. As Sergeant Biggs worked to block the exits of the convict's hideout, he "observed the approach of the other patrol," and according to Tench "realized that if he and his detail were to receive the credit of recapturing Casshel he must work fast."

Cooperation within the close-knit fraternity of officers never turned into corruption. The NWMP and its successor in 1920, the Royal Canadian Mounted Police, were particularly scrupulous about not showing any favour toward their members. The scarlet uniform granted no immunity when it came to wrongdoing. For instance, steely-eyed J. D. Nicholson lost his sergeant's stripes for a mistake made by a greenhorn constable under his command. The three officers on duty when Casshel made his break were dismissed from the force and received jail time, evidence that "the discipline of the Mounted Police is adamant. No extenuating circumstances are allowed to weaken it."

In the hands of Canada's pulp writers, occasional lapses like these were what drove the mounteds' ultimate success. "His right sleeve showing brighter where three golden chevrons and a star had been removed," Nicholson burned with "a cold anger" and, according to Philip Godsell, redoubled his efforts to capture the murderer. For Tench, the NWMP's uncompromising treatment of its members was "what makes the force what it is — perhaps the finest disciplined body of men in the world."

GETTING THEIR MAN

Nowhere was that discipline more apparent than in the actual pursuit of criminals. The idea that working hard and working smart were the foundations of

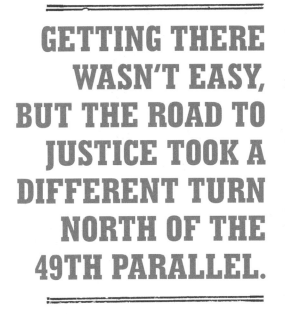

GETTING THERE WASN'T EASY, BUT THE ROAD TO JUSTICE TOOK A DIFFERENT TURN NORTH OF THE 49TH PARALLEL.

C. D. C.
FEBRUARY
Feature
DETECTIVE
cases
25¢
A Girl's Road to Disaster

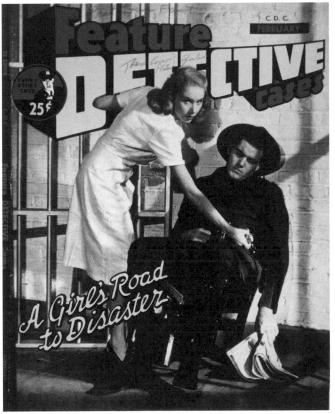

police power emerged from the structure of true crime stories as much as their content, which emphasized the challenges confronting lawmen and the painstaking work of detection. These police procedurals weren't mystery stories but accounts of police work where the investigation was centre stage. This genre has a genealogy stretching back to the 19th century, but the police procedural enjoyed enormous popularity during the Second World War.

Even before the exploits of Sergeant Joe Friday were available on television's Dragnet, avid Canadian readers could satisfy their voyeuristic desires for an inside look at investigations by grabbing a true crime magazine

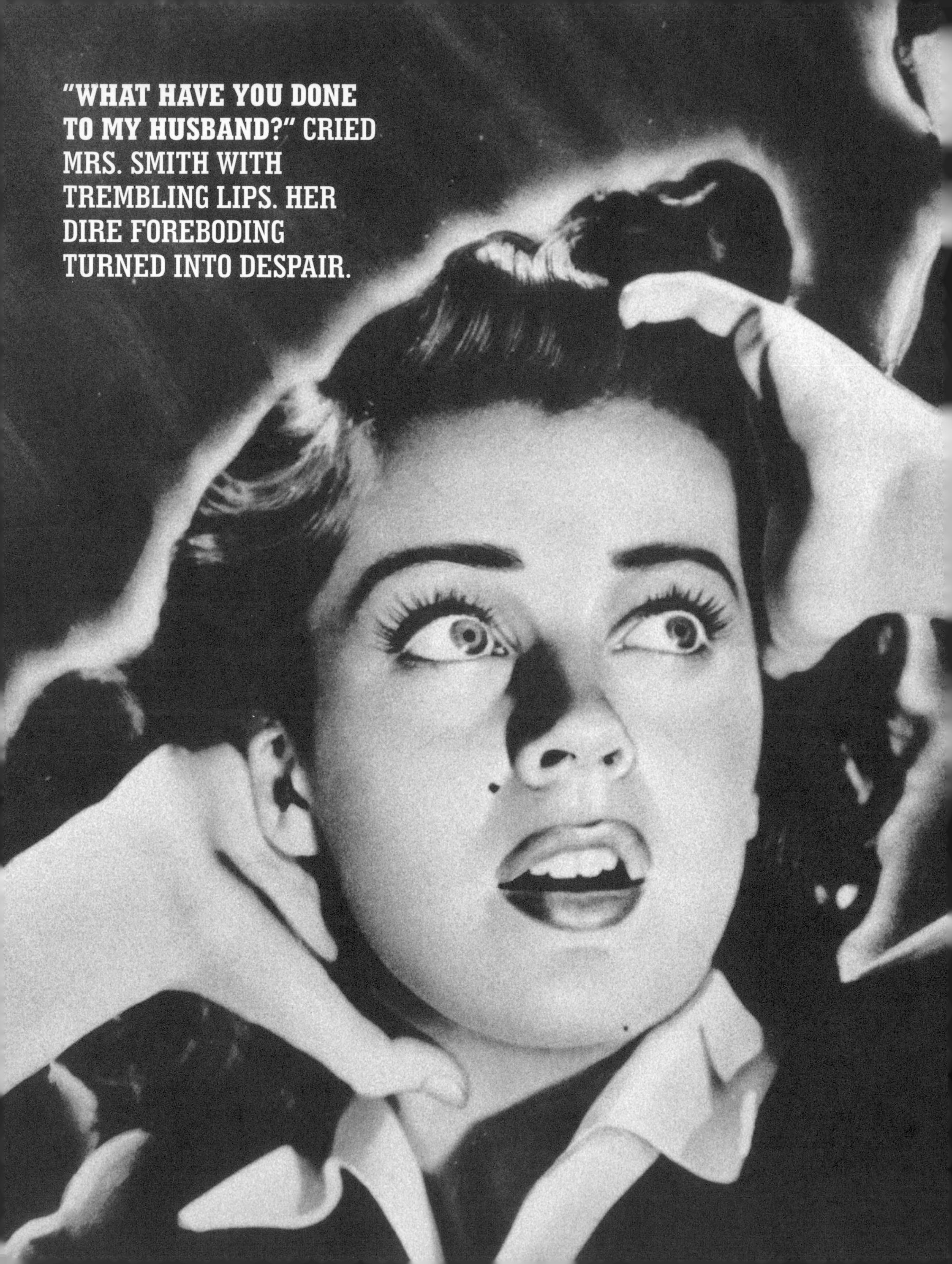
"WHAT HAVE YOU DONE TO MY HUSBAND?" CRIED MRS. SMITH WITH TREMBLING LIPS. HER DIRE FOREBODING TURNED INTO DESPAIR.

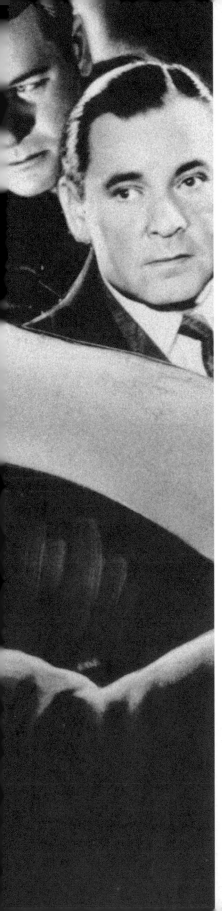

from the newsstand. The story titles alone betrayed their point of view. When the police weren't "Trailing the _____ (fill in the blank: e.g. Phantom Killers, Firebrand of the Rockies, Notorious Baker Gang)," they were "Solving the _____ (fill in the blank: e.g., B.C. Sandpit Mystery)" or chasing "The Clue of the _____ (fill in the blank: e.g. Chinese Bowl, Homemade Blackjack, Cloven Skull)." Stories like these took readers on the job with the investigating officers, plodding relentlessly toward the solution of the crime and the capture of the criminal.

True crime writers revealed the evidence to readers in the same way it would have been revealed to the police. Sometimes they did this by writing in the first person but more commonly true crime stories were narrated in the third person, giving readers a sense of being there, seeing the scene alongside the police. "As spades bit into the soft earth they exposed a headless body, still in a good state of preservation, clad in jean overalls, heavy boots and a dark tweed coat. The overalls bore a Kansas City tag." Passages like this reinforced the identification between the police and the readers at the same time they revealed the process by which offenders were brought to justice.

Getting there was never easy, but the road to justice took a different turn north of the 49th parallel. Unlike the majority of British and American police procedurals, which led readers through the seamy streets of London, Glasgow, New York or Los Angeles, Canadian true crime stories had cops trailing suspects through the country's wilderness precincts, introducing their audiences to places like Herschel Island, Fort Nelson, Aklavik and Norway House, places of adventure and danger in the True North.

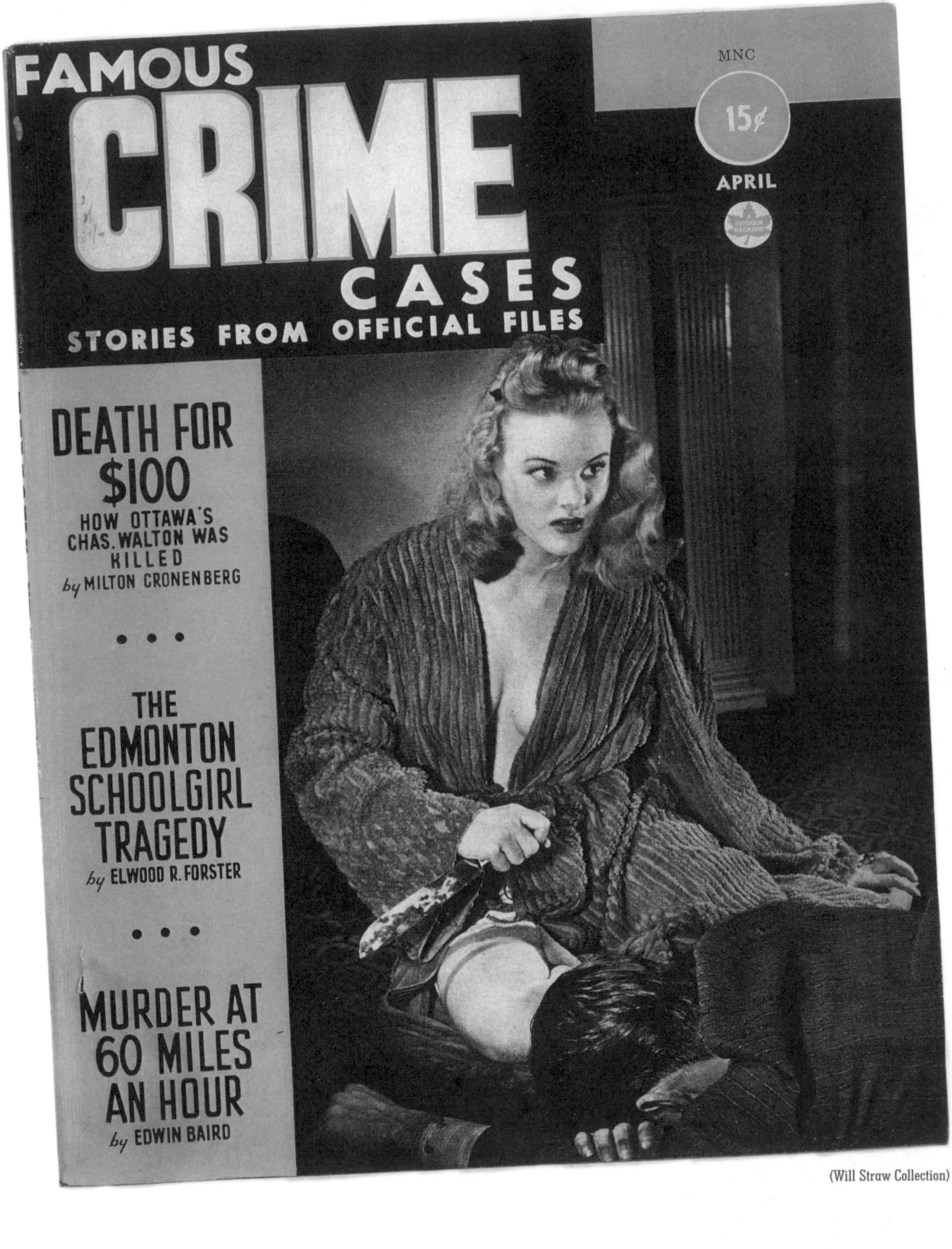
FAMOUS
CRIME
CASES
STORIES FROM OFFICIAL FILES
MNC
15¢
APRIL
DEATH FOR
$100
HOW OTTAWA'S
CHAS. WALTON WAS
KILLED
by MILTON CRONENBERG
THE
EDMONTON
SCHOOLGIRL
TRAGEDY
by ELWOOD R. FORSTER
MURDER AT
60 MILES
AN HOUR
by EDWIN BAIRD
(Will Straw Collection)

If the amount of space devoted to describing their formidable qualities is any indication, venues like these posed a greater challenge to Canada's finest and were more fully developed as features in true crime stories than were the criminals themselves. According to Philip Godsell, Fort Nelson, a "lonely Hudson's Bay Company fur post deep in the fastnesses of British Columbia," was so isolated that it drove the B.C. Provincial Police stationed there to pine for the "bright lights" — of Edmonton!

True crime stories created a moral geography for Canada linking violence and depravity to particular places — like Whitehorse, for instance. In 1901, apparently, "robbery and murder were the order of the day."

Shots were exchanged in broad daylight on the streets. At night the crash of tinny orchestras and the cracked voices of bedizened harlots mingled at times with cries of "Murder!" In the dance halls straw haired bo-crushers tripped the light fantastic at a dollar a set and a percentage on the drinks, while now and then some poor devil would be found lying lifeless across his rifled sled — powder marks on his back and his pockets inside out.

Places like Fort St. John, Whitehorse and the Klondike were so evocative that a good rendering of them could rescue an otherwise weak true crime tale. In pitching "Icy Hell" to the publishers of *True Detective*, Philip Godsell admitted that his story about the murder of an American sportsman-scientist by Inuit "lacked one thing — the murderers weren't hanged, or even imprisoned." "To make up for this," he promised to "work up … highlights … on the perseverance of the police in contesting their puny might with the forces of Nature."

If as a police officer you could outwit Mother Nature, unravelling human nature would be a snap — provided your mind was as disciplined as your body. For Canadian true crime writers, bringing offenders to justice was more about close observation and hard work than forensic science. Perhaps in keeping with the geography of crime in the Canadian pulps, there were relatively few references to forensic laboratories, fingerprinting, blood-typing, or the use of photography to document a crime scene.

ACCORDING TO PHILIP GODSELL, FORT NELSON, A "LONELY HUDSON'S BAY COMPANY FUR POST DEEP IN THE FASTNESSES OF BRITISH COLUMBIA," WAS SO ISOLATED THAT IT DROVE THE B.C. PROVINCIAL POLICE STATIONED THERE TO PINE FOR THE "BRIGHT LIGHTS" — OF EDMONTON!

ROBBERY AND MURDER WERE THE ORDER OF THE DAY.

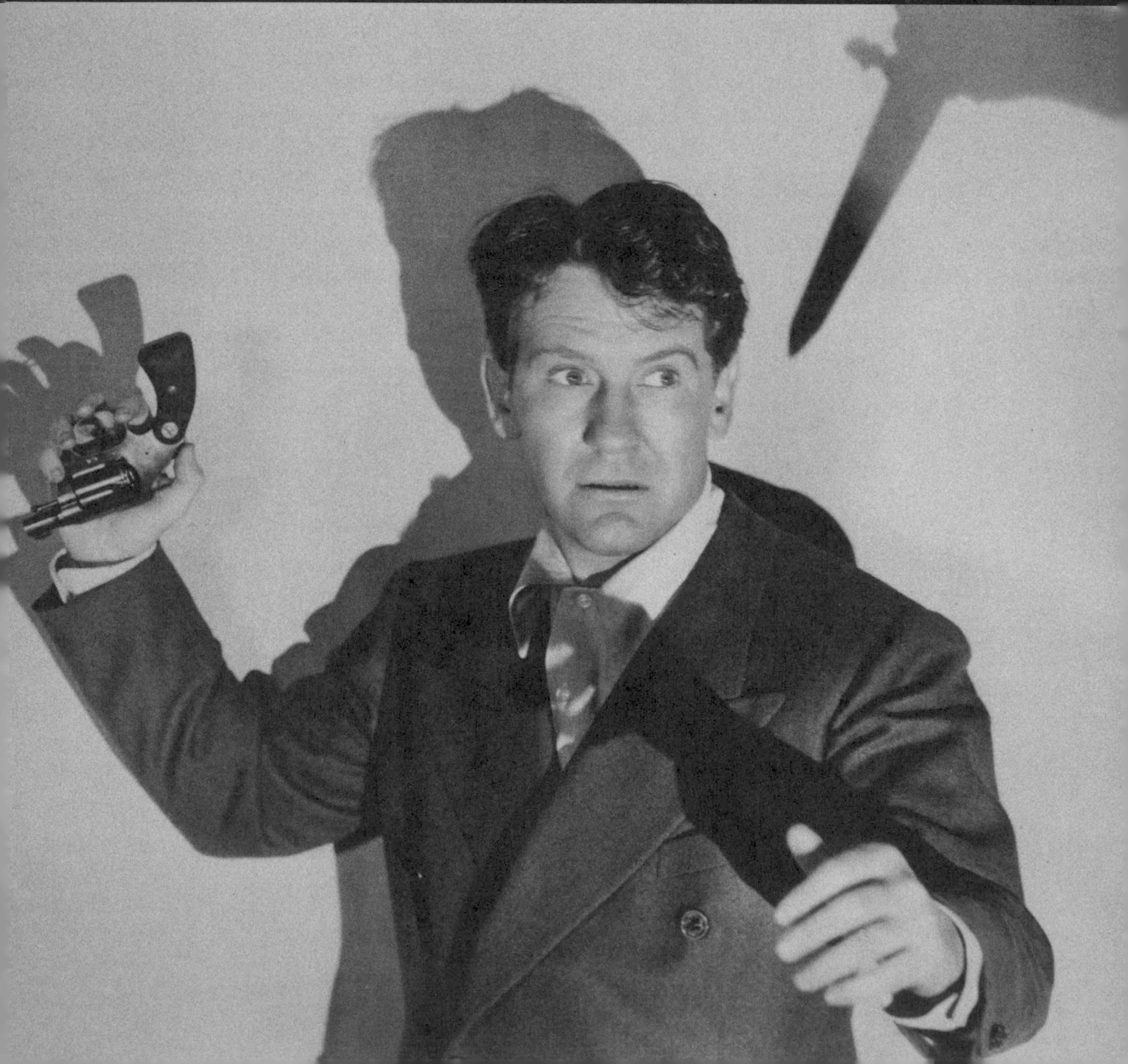

Instead, travelling around on horseback, by dogsled or in police canoes, Mounties and Provincials solved crimes with little more than some string and a magnifying glass. Such was the case in "The Mystery of the Screaming Target," C. V. Tench's story of how Constable Sheard solved the 1933 shooting death of Annie Wolenski. Using a borrowed ball of binder twine, the Alberta Provincial Police constable was able to determine where the shooter had stood by extrapolating back from two bullet holes in the Wolenski farmhouse. The split and spent shell casings at the site provided important clues, only recognizable to a "trained mind." According to Tench, "those tiny splits in the brass told Sheard … that the cartridges had been fired from a rifle a mere fraction too large for them! Such a rifle would be a British .303 calibre. That narrowed the search down."

Sometimes the only equipment an officer needed to crack a case was dogged determination, as in Philip Godsell's "Clue of the Shrinking Corpse." When a badly decomposed body was found in a shallow grave outside Ponoka, Alberta, all the Mounties were able to ascertain immediately was that he was an American who had been shot to death by a Smith and Wesson .38. With "no other clues than the almost unrecognizable visage of the dead man, a greasy cap, and a Leisure Hour [Magazine] Library," Corporal Hetherington of the mounted scoured the countryside asking questions, only "to be rewarded with vacant faces, or to be sent on useless trails by yokels giving false information just to please or be polite." Eventually, however, police efforts (aided by another piece of string) paid off, and Hetherington and his partner managed to weave a noose around the neck of a callous killer.

Persistence was the foundation of the Mounties' success, but it never hurt to have an idiot savant on the force. In W. W. Bride's "Trailing the Phantom Killers," a story about the 1933 hunt for the murderers of bachelor farmer Walter Parsille, "hundreds of leads were turned in and investigated," but for naught. The Albertan's killers were caught only when "a young and alert officer of the Mounties" in neighbouring Saskatchewan made the connection between a pair of transient harvest workers in his district and the information and description contained in an old all-points bulletin. Apparently the youthful Constable Ashby had "made a practice of memorizing the faces, names, and facts contained in the circulars," explaining that "you can never tell when they would be useful."

As important as shoe leather, elbow grease and good powers of deduction were to fighting crime, true crime cops also relied on their

TRAILING THE ELUSIVE TENCH

While the crimes that inspired stories are possible to trace through court records, finding anything about the scribes who put them there is much harder. Authors often concealed their identities. C. V. Tench wrote using his own name, but also under several pseudonyms, including Jack Lunter, Charles Truscott and Ned Ward. But perhaps his most intriguing nom de pulp was William Brockie, "Ex-Sergeant" of the RCMP. Whether he knew it or not, impersonating a police officer was a criminal offence "against the administration of law and justice."

enormous fund of local knowledge and deep understanding of human nature to save the day. Most officers were like Constable Sheard, who was "more or less familiar with the history of everyone in his district." When confronted with a crime, the first thing he did was to "mentally con over what he knew" of the victims and their associates. Rather than rely on

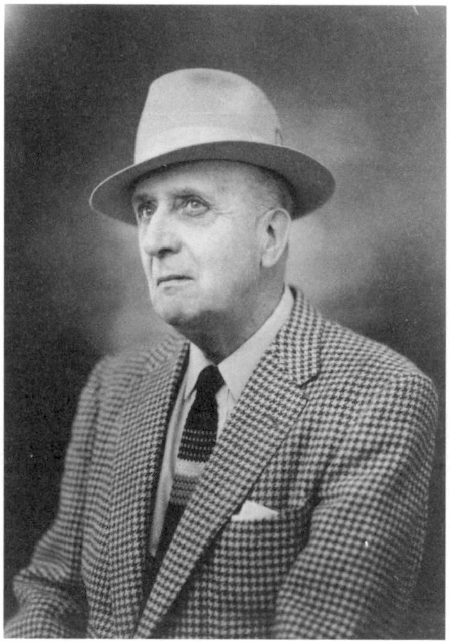

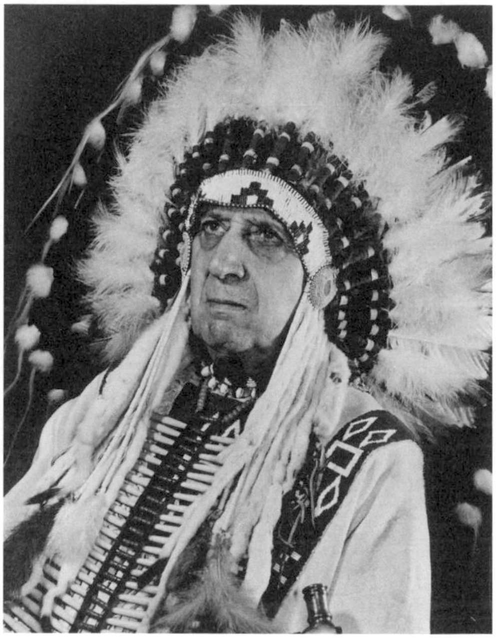

One of Canada's most prolific true crime writers, Philip Godsell (1889–1961) never met an adjective he didn't like. His stories were full of "mahogany-faced" savages and "steely-eyed" Mounties matching wits with each other in the "empurpled" dusk of the prairie skies or in the "shade of the saw-toothed mountains" of British Columbia. An auditor by trade, he preferred to be known as "Philip H. Godsell, FRGS. Arctic Traveller, Author, and Explorer."

(Philip H. Godsell Fonds, Glenbow Library, Calgary Alberta)

such local knowledge to track down an escaped prisoner, Sergeant Nicholson put an old piece of folk wisdom to work. According to Philip Godsell, "recalling the French adage *cherchez la femme*, he proceeded to probe for the woman in [the prisoner's] life" and had the man in custody in no time.

In the Far North and Arctic especially, the knowledge that successful officers possessed was both environmental and ethnographic. Studying the wooden poles lashed to a body found floating in the Yukon River, Sergeant McLauchlin "noticed that one was a spruce pole; two were green willows; two were the Balm of Gilead and the other an alder." Because "it wasn't everywhere that such an assortment of growth could be found," locating the scene of the crime was an easy task for the woodsman-Mountie. For C. V. Tench, unravelling cases involving Inuit required the police to become amateur anthropologists, experts in the behaviour and beliefs of their "savage" and "child-like" charges. A Mountie stationed in the Arctic quickly learned that though "fair-minded and good natured for the most part, an Eskimo rarely takes a human life, but when he does turn killer he stops at nothing." The motivation was often the "keen competition for wives" brought on by the "great shortage of marriageable girls among these Northern nomads."

IN THE FAR NORTH AND ARCTIC ESPECIALLY, THE KNOWLEDGE THAT SUCCESSFUL OFFICERS POSSESSED WAS BOTH ENVIRONMENTAL AND ETHNOGRAPHIC.

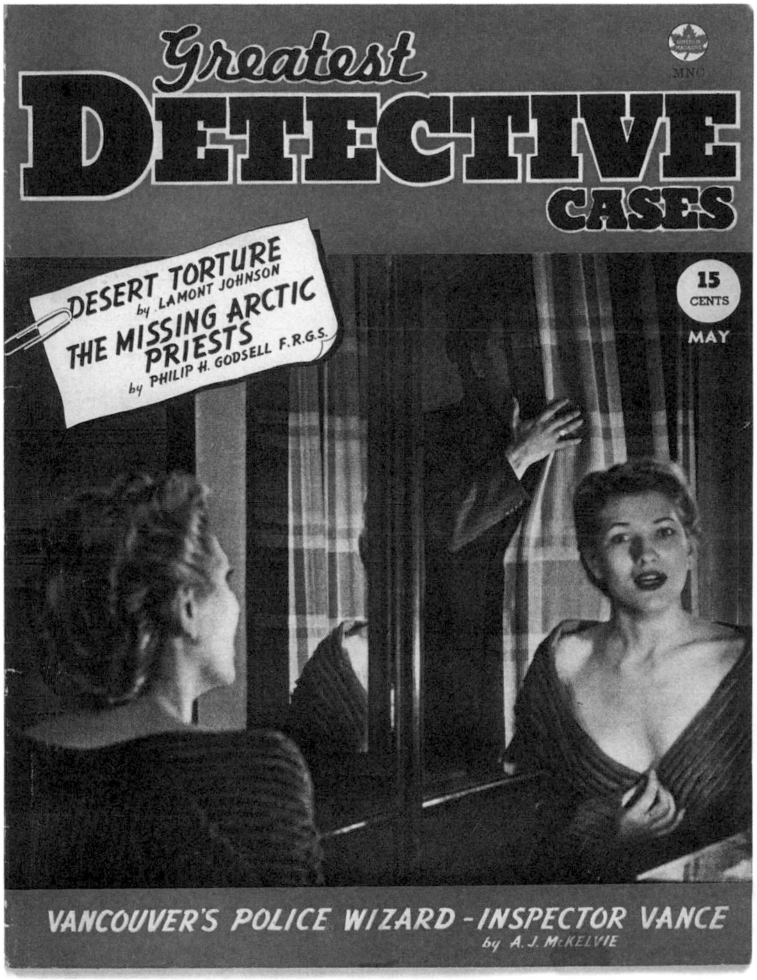
Greatest
DETECTIVE
CASES
MNC
15 CENTS
MAY
DESERT TORTURE by LAMONT JOHNSON
THE MISSING ARCTIC PRIESTS by PHILIP H. GODSELL F.R.G.S.
VANCOUVER'S POLICE WIZARD - INSPECTOR VANCE
by A. J. McKELVIE

(Will Straw Collection)

FROM GETTING IT RIGHT TO MAINTAINING THE RIGHT

The singularly positive picture of lawmen (and especially the mounted variety) painted in Canada's true crime magazines set these police procedurals apart from their American and British counterparts, which often portrayed individual officers and the practice of law enforcement in a more complex way, casting them in darker light, or at least one that made it possible for readers to discern shades of grey between good and evil.

Stories like these also exemplified the Mounties' growing self-consciousness about public relations. Although the RCMP had always enforced strict regulations to preserve their stalwart image, it wasn't until the 1950s that the force began to take an active role in regulating the nature and circulation of its use, attempting to control everything from View Master slides of uniformed officers to postcards, and eventually to television series.

Until that time, the Mounties and other police forces benefited from the uniformly positive press they received in the pages of the pulps, something they had a direct role in creating. Philip Godsell, the most prolific of English Canada's true crime writers in the 1940s, routinely submitted his stories to the RCMP and various provincial police commissioners and the chiefs of municipal forces for comment before they were published. In his view, doing so improved his stories' veracity and authenticity — not to mention their market value.

Oftentimes, however, the police were Godsell's harshest critics, taking him to task for factual errors in an attempt to fashion what they considered to be a "true representation of the Force." For instance, B.C. Provincial Police commissioner T. W. Parsons returned one of Godsell's manuscripts in 1941, noting that because it "contained a great many inaccuracies" the officer involved "strongly objects to having his name appear in it at all … I would certainly suggest that you make further check on details of this case before offering it for publication."

Superintendent A. H. L. Mellor, who was assistant director of the RCMP's Criminal Investigation Branch, took issue with Godsell's characterization of a Mountie inspector. "You have made Inspector Anderson somewhat of a comical character," Mellor wrote. "Although Anderson did not talk perfect English, he certainly did not speak a mixture of broken Swedish and English as it appears from your story, and it is suggested you might correct this, as in its present state it somewhat weakens the effect of your otherwise excellent account …"

Other uniformed consultants, such as Commander E. C. P. Salt of Charlottetown's L Division, took exception to the conventions of the true crime genre. "I am returning your script with the candid statement that I dislike anything of this nature," Salt told Godsell in 1939. Nonetheless, in accordance with the commissioner's request Salt did agree to help. "My purpose in sending you this 'Brief' is that you will not do that which is so objectionable in the part of many writers. Make a hero of one member of the Force at the expense of the others. My objection to provide material to writers is that there is a tendency on the part of the writer to glorify the individual work rather than the 'team' work."

The Mounties' willingness to act as amateur true crime editors stemmed from their recognition that their effectiveness depended largely on the public's perception of them as a collective, impartial force for good that relied on intelligence and painstaking police work. By the middle of the 20th century, the Mounties' reputation alone was apparently enough to bring bad guys to justice in the pulps. With images of the relentless Corporal Brainard pushing him on, Craven began to take risks to put even more distance between himself and the Mountie, triggering an avalanche that took his life. Ironically, as C. V. Tench concluded, Brainard hadn't a clue that a crime had been committed, much less knew who the perpetrator was. In his view, Craven had been the "victim of panic" brought on by a guilty conscience and his fear of the force's formidable reputation, something that transcended even the daunting powers of its individual officers.

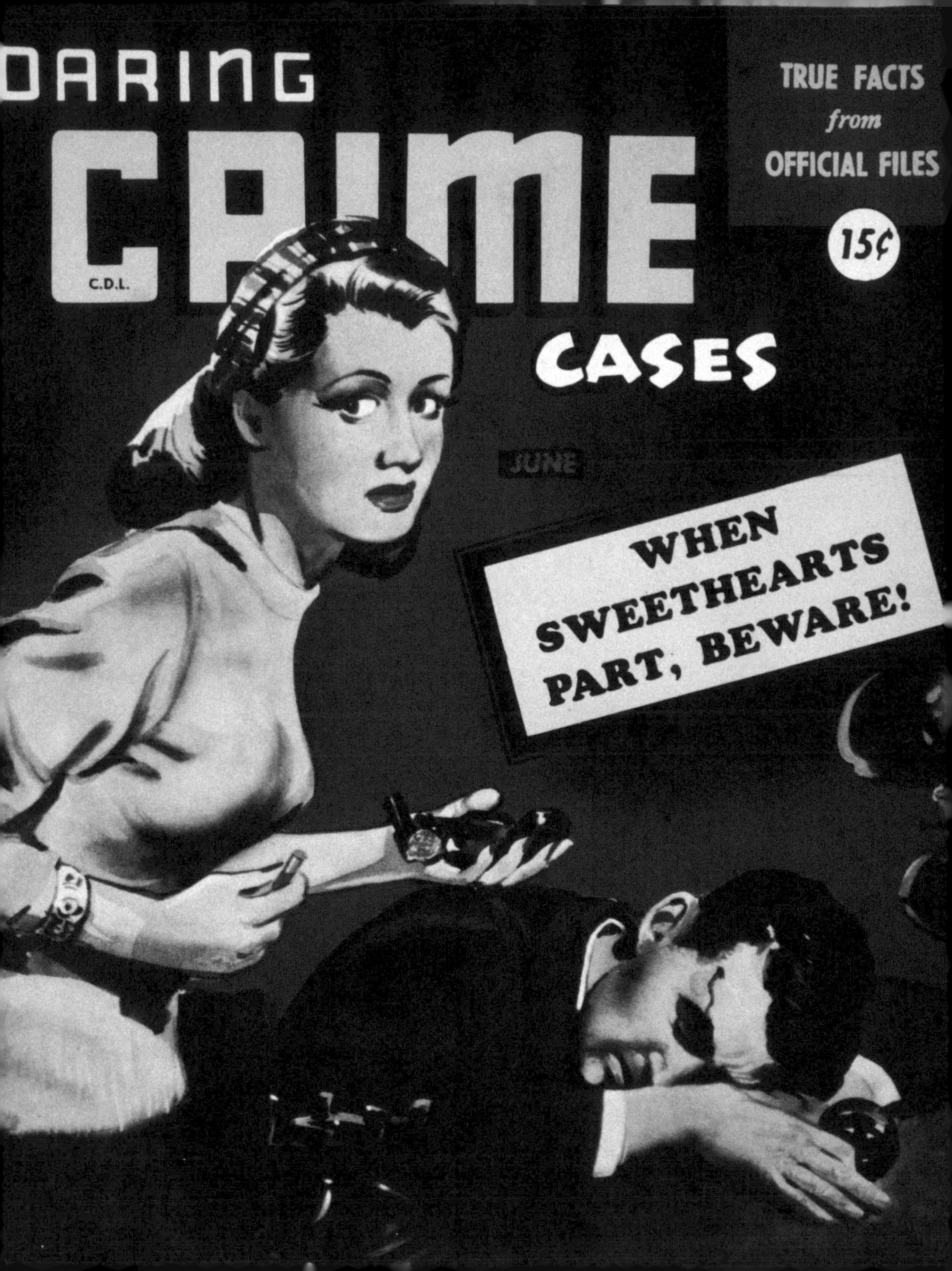

DARING
CRIME
C.D.L.
CASES
TRUE FACTS
from
OFFICIAL FILES
15¢
JUNE
WHEN SWEETHEARTS PART, BEWARE!

3

LOVE GONE WRONG

A FINE ROMANCE, a fairy-tale wedding and marital bliss … Canadians were no different from their American counterparts when it came to fantasizing about the prospect of a happy union. The Depression had forced many to put off plans for marriage. Then Canada joined Britain in the Second World War, forcing women to wave goodbye to their sweethearts.

If the shaky national economy and the winds of war knocked many Canadians' domestic arrangements awry in the 1930s and '40s, true crime magazines assured readers that some things never changed, including the mysteries of heterosexual attraction. Advertisements for such classics as *Confessions of a Gorgeous Hussy* and *When a Red-Blooded Man Must Say Yes* appeared regularly in the pulps. So did ads for books geared toward readers keen to find mates and settle down (*How to Meet Men and Marry* apparently provided step-by-step instructions).

True crime stories never questioned the magnetic pull between men and women, but they did explore the tragic aftermath of love gone wrong. The typical cover — a barely clad, busty woman — left little doubt that the prime ingredient for romantic disaster was untamed sexual passion. Although most prosecuted homicides (then as now) involve men's violence toward other men, true crime magazine covers gave the impression that every murder involved a deadly love triangle or an enraged lover. Like pulp fiction magazines such as *The Black Mask* and Hollywood film noir movies such as *Gun Crazy* and *Double Indemnity*, true crime pulp covers lured readers with sexy images of femmes fatales and female victims. As one magazine warned, "WHEN SWEETHEARTS PART, BEWARE!"

Real cases of marital and romantic discord tended to be far less colourful than pulp magazine covers suggested, however. And the stories were

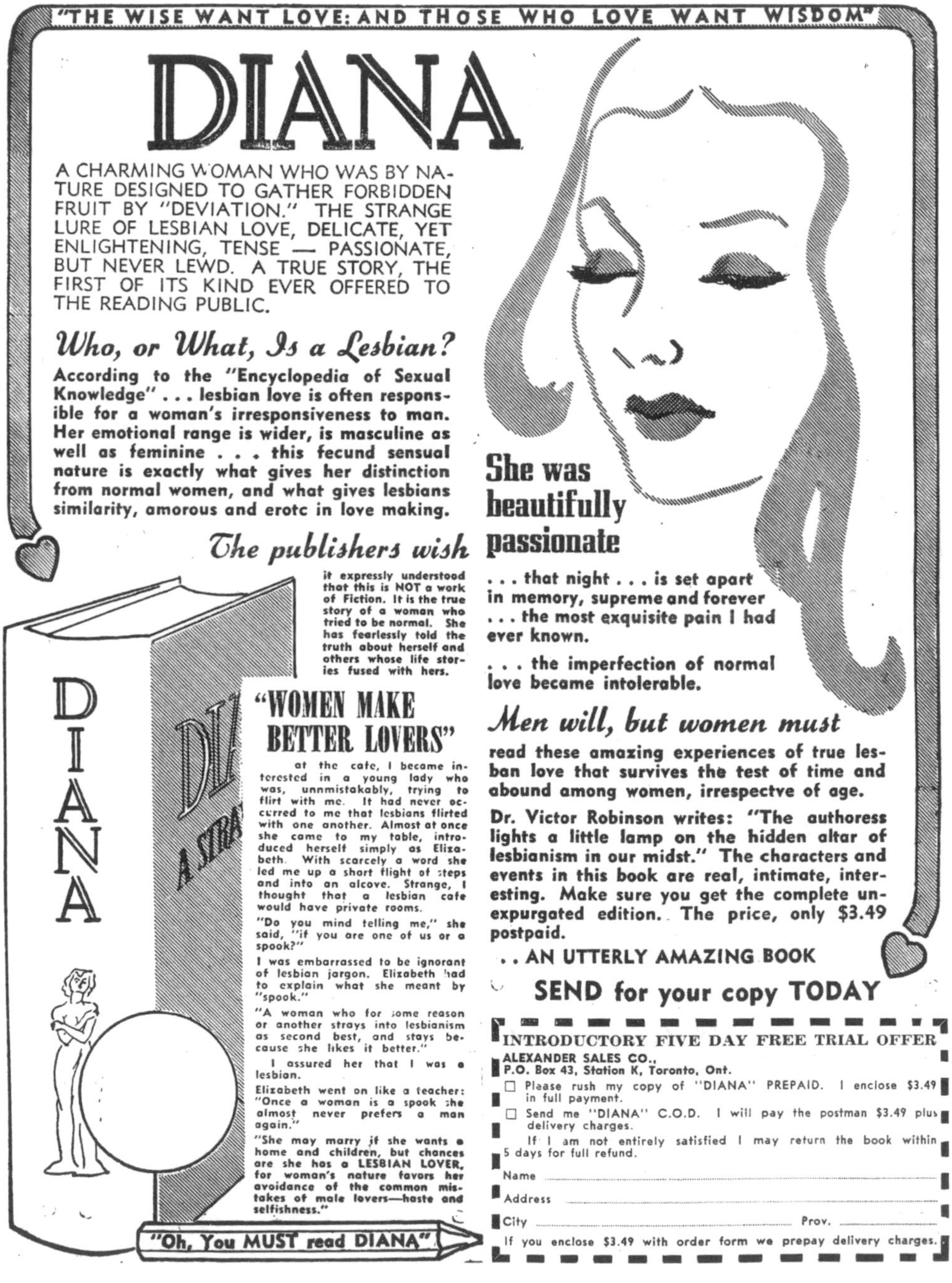
"THE WISE WANT LOVE: AND THOSE WHO LOVE WANT WISDOM"
DIANA
A CHARMING WOMAN WHO WAS BY NATURE DESIGNED TO GATHER FORBIDDEN FRUIT BY "DEVIATION." THE STRANGE LURE OF LESBIAN LOVE, DELICATE, YET ENLIGHTENING, TENSE — PASSIONATE, BUT NEVER LEWD. A TRUE STORY, THE FIRST OF ITS KIND EVER OFFERED TO THE READING PUBLIC.
Who, or What, Is a Lesbian?
According to the "Encyclopedia of Sexual Knowledge" . . . lesbian love is often responsible for a woman's irresponsiveness to man. Her emotional range is wider, is masculine as well as feminine . . . this fecund sensual nature is exactly what gives her distinction from normal women, and what gives lesbians similarity, amorous and erotc in love making.
The publishers wish
it expressly understood that this is NOT a work of Fiction. It is the true story of a woman who tried to be normal. She has fearlessly told the truth about herself and others whose life stories fused with hers.
She was beautifully passionate
. . . that night . . . is set apart in memory, supreme and forever . . . the most exquisite pain I had ever known.
. . . the imperfection of normal love became intolerable.
Men will, but women must
read these amazing experiences of true lesban love that survives the test of time and abound among women, irrespectve of age.
Dr. Victor Robinson writes: "The authoress lights a little lamp on the hidden altar of lesbianism in our midst." The characters and events in this book are real, intimate, interesting. Make sure you get the complete unexpurgated edition. The price, only $3.49 postpaid.
. . AN UTTERLY AMAZING BOOK
SEND for your copy TODAY
DIANA
"WOMEN MAKE BETTER LOVERS"
at the cafe, I became interested in a young lady who was, unnmistakably, trying to flirt with me. It had never occurred to me that lesbians flirted with one another. Almost at once she came to my table, introduced herself simply as Elizabeth. With scarcely a word she led me up a short flight of steps and into an alcove. Strange, I thought that a lesbian cafe would have private rooms.
"Do you mind telling me," she said, "if you are one of us or a spook?"
I was embarrassed to be ignorant of lesbian jargon. Elizabeth had to explain what she meant by "spook."
"A woman who for some reason or another strays into lesbianism as second best, and stays because she likes it better."
I assured her that I was a lesbian.
Elizabeth went on like a teacher: "Once a woman is a spook she almost never prefers a man again."
"She may marry if she wants a home and children, but chances are she has a LESBIAN LOVER, for woman's nature favors her avoidance of the common mistakes of male lovers—haste and selfishness."
"Oh, You MUST read DIANA"
INTRODUCTORY FIVE DAY FREE TRIAL OFFER
ALEXANDER SALES CO.,
P.O. Box 43, Station K, Toronto, Ont.
Please rush my copy of "DIANA" PREPAID. I enclose $3.49 in full payment.
Send me "DIANA" C.O.D. I will pay the postman $3.49 plus delivery charges.
If I am not entirely satisfied I may return the book within 5 days for full refund.
Name
Address
City
Prov.
If you enclose $3.49 with order form we prepay delivery charges.

DIANA: THE AUTOBIOGRAPHY OF A STRANGE, WAYWARD WOMAN Ads for Diana ran in the true crime pulps, raising the question: "Who or What Is a Lesbian?" Promising "to call a spade a spade," the book answered "in dramatic fashion such questions as: 'What did my wife do while I was at the front?'; "Will my wartime marriage last?'; 'What to do about the problems of social diseases.'" What price love? The Alexander Sales Company knew.

downright conservative when it came to depicting heterosexual attraction and its ugly consequences. Condemning romantic excess in any form, pulp writers explored the tragic results of extramarital affairs and passionate liaisons that could unhinge even a tightly buttoned Anglo-Canadian. There was nothing distinctly Canadian about failed romances that ended in murder, but there were notably Canadian variations on this well-worn true crime

How To
Meet Men and Marry

By JULIET FARNHAM

This book goes far beyond any book ever published. It is the frankest, most practical book for women ever written.

What should the Pre-Marriage relationship be? Do you have trouble in holding your dates?

Do you know how to turn new acquaintances into a romance?

Do you find difficulty in meeting new men?

What keeps men from marrying?

These and hundreds of other questions are answered, not in generalities but in specific detail.

WAR and MAN . . . What new angles enter into the "WAR OF THE SEXES" with the advent of Global War?

Here are new obstacles to overcome, the allure of European women, how to maintain the interest of your man when he is overseas.

Mrs. Juliet Farnham shows a brilliant insight —the outcome of deep study—into the problems of romance and gives clear, plain and simple answers to all its varied problems.

Women—You have the weapons, learn to use them.

Get the answers to your ROMANCE PROBLEMS in this brilliantly written book.

SHIPPED PREPAID $2.49

ALEXANDER SALES COMPANY

SUITE 304   95 KING ST. EAST

TORONTO, ONTARIO, CANADA

HOW TO MEET MEN AND MARRY
By the Second World War, keeping the home fires burning required much more than matches. Single women needed to launch new offensives, while those who were attached needed to ensure their defences were up to foreign assaults. A manual titled How to Meet Men and Marry that was advertised in the back of some pulps promised to help women "turn new acquaintances into a romance."

theme. Publisher Al Valentine favoured stories of domestic disasters that had put police to the test — killings in remote northern communities or murders that occurred within Canada's foreign "colonies" and Native communities. Wherever they trekked, they always ended up exploring the universal tragedy of love's capacity to turn into hate.

"Is your marriage a flop?" a book advertisement in *Women and Crime* inquired. For readers who privately answered "yes," stories of domestic homicide provided guilty pleasures. For anyone who secretly wondered what life might be like without a dreary mate, stories of love gone wrong could transport them to settings where women aimed and pulled the trigger, where men wrapped their fingers around their lovers' necks and squeezed.

'CAUSE A MAN'S GOT NEEDS

Love triangles have always inspired writers of fiction, from Shakespeare to Spillane. In the world of Canadian true crime, passions were sometimes their hottest where the weather was coldest — not in the big cities of the south, but in the tiny communities and outposts that dotted the Great White North.

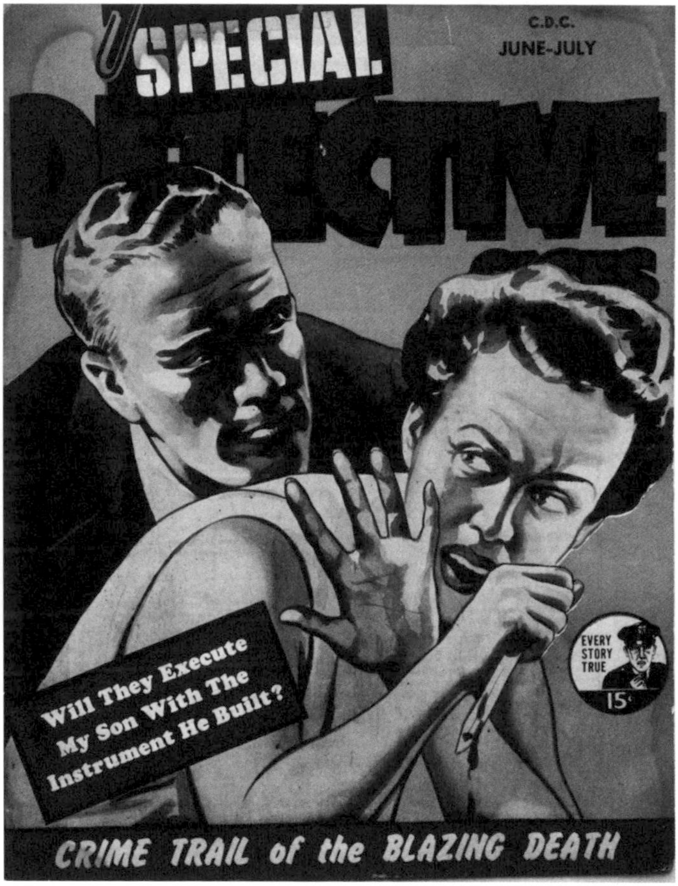
SPECIAL
DETECTIVE
C.D.C.
JUNE-JULY
Will They Execute My Son With The Instrument He Built?
EVERY STORY TRUE
15¢
CRIME TRAIL of the BLAZING DEATH

FOR ANYONE WHO SECRETLY WONDERED WHAT LIFE MIGHT BE LIKE WITHOUT A DREARY MATE, STORIES OF LOVE GONE WRONG COULD TRANSPORT THEM TO SETTINGS WHERE WOMEN AIMED AND PULLED THE TRIGGER, WHERE MEN WRAPPED THEIR FINGERS AROUND THEIR LOVERS' NECKS AND SQUEEZED.

Isolation and interminable dark, cold nights could become hothouse environments for the green-eyed monster. Petty jealousies and imagined slights erased the closest of male friendships and snapped the bonds of matrimony. According to Canadian pulp writers, men had certain needs that just had to be satisfied … even at absolute zero.

The case of trappers John Harms and his buddy "Little Johnny" Anthony certainly provided all the right ingredients. The men were business partners, reportedly the best of friends, who eked out a living on Singing Dog

Island in Lake Athabasca, which straddles the Alberta-Saskatchewan border and is not everyone's idea of paradise, but was close enough for these freedom-loving mountain men. In "Death in the North," published in *Dare Devil Detective*, Neil Perrin wrote that "they had lived together in perfect harmony" for two years … *"and then there came a woman."*

Her name was Ann Lindgren. Hired as a housekeeper by another trapper in the Athabasca region, the "comely" woman immediately attracted her distant neighbours' attention. The elder man, Harms, was instantly smitten and "Little Johnny" knew it. North of 60, Cupid's arrow hit with the force of a poleaxe, especially if a man had been drinking. Well-lubricated and lovesick, Harms began "to talk entirely too much of things that are better not on a man's mind in the long winters on Lake Athabaska."

The object of Harms' drunken attention found him as appealing as a dead skunk. She tried to avoid him on her regular visits to Fort Chipewyan, not an easy thing to do in a one-street town. When his partner suggested that they stop paying visits to the woman, Harms suspected the worst: "'Little Johnny' wanted Ann Lindgren for himself!"

Here the story took a predictable turn: "A jealous smouldering rage" grew in him and "wild, primitive urges" drove him to shoot his partner dead, in spite of the woman's pleas. Harms decided to take her by force.

Unlike the barely clad women on the true crime covers, Ann Lindgren was well wrapped and resourceful. Barricading herself in her cabin with nothing but her wits and an old hunting rifle, she managed to fend off the "drink-sodden, lust-crazed trapper." In true red-serge fashion, the Mounties arrived in the nick of time and saved the day without further loss of life. Shooting only to disarm the man, Sergeant Vernon placed the "unkempt and wild-eyed" Harms under arrest.

While most true crime stories featured murder cases in which the perpetrator had been executed, this 1935 case had a tender tone that might have appealed to readers who picked up a copy of *True Confessions* along with their *Dare Devil Detective*. Lindgren was no femme fatale; in fact, the woman who had unwittingly stirred up jealousy redeemed herself as an angel of mercy. Her testimony that homebrew had driven Harms to kill didn't convince the jury but it did provide fodder for a successful plea before the Saskatchewan Court of Appeal (having future prime minister John Diefenbaker for a lawyer didn't hurt his chances, either). Retried and convicted on the lesser charge of manslaughter, Harms still had to pay a stiff "penalty for the hatred engendered when

'Little Johnny' Anthony looked at the same woman he desired."

Fatal lust triangles were actually more likely to end in the death of the woman, not male rivals. This was true in real life as well as in the cases that writers selected for true crime material. For all the cover images of tough broads, the pulps' contents confirmed that women who played with fire got burned.

Such was the fate of "tantalizing" Margaret Poole, whose husband flew into a jealous rage and killed her when he found her "whirling in the arms" of another trapper at a midwinter dance. The same fate befell 16-year-old Pearl Dell, who rebuffed a "harmless, gently-smiling middle-aged" Manitoba hired hand's attentions. When he discovered that she had given her heart to another, the mild-mannered man turned into a "lust-crazed slashing slayer," according to W. W. Bride.

No matter how beastly their attackers, the women in these stories were typically blamed for stirring up men's passions. Margaret Poole "lacked domestic obedience," while young Pearl Dell had the poor judgement to take an unchaperoned car ride with a single man. Even Ann Lindgren had a mysterious past. What had drawn a "comely" woman with a two-year-old "babe" into the company of northern trappers?

WHAT'S BRED IN THE BONE

True crime writers took their creative cues from other art forms popular in the era, particularly pulp fiction and Hollywood melodramas and adventure films. The crimes they wrote about involved people with complex emotions and motivations, but once rendered into true crime characters, their images were taken straight out of central casting. Women were vixens or victims, the completely innocent female victim being a rarity. Ethnic and racial pigeon-holing and pidgin English provided shorthand, two-dimensional characterizations. If white trappers could fly off the handle in the north, Indians, French Canadians and blacks, as well as Southern and Eastern Europeans were congenitally prone to jealousy.

The "Indian," a stock figure in every Hollywood Western, was more likely in the Canadian pulps to be the insanely jealous type, rather than a stoic figure or a warrior. Pulp Natives locked in love triangles were possessed of short fuses and hot passions. Accounts of broken hearts and dead bodies in Canada's North and West confirmed what southern white readers already thought they knew about indigenous people: they were driven by passion to crime.

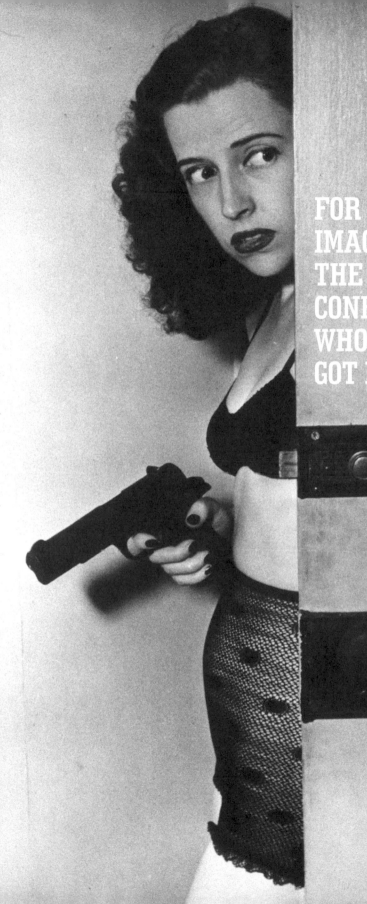

FOR ALL THE COVER IMAGES OF TOUGH BROADS, THE PULPS' CONTENTS CONFIRMED THAT WOMEN WHO PLAYED WITH FIRE GOT BURNED.

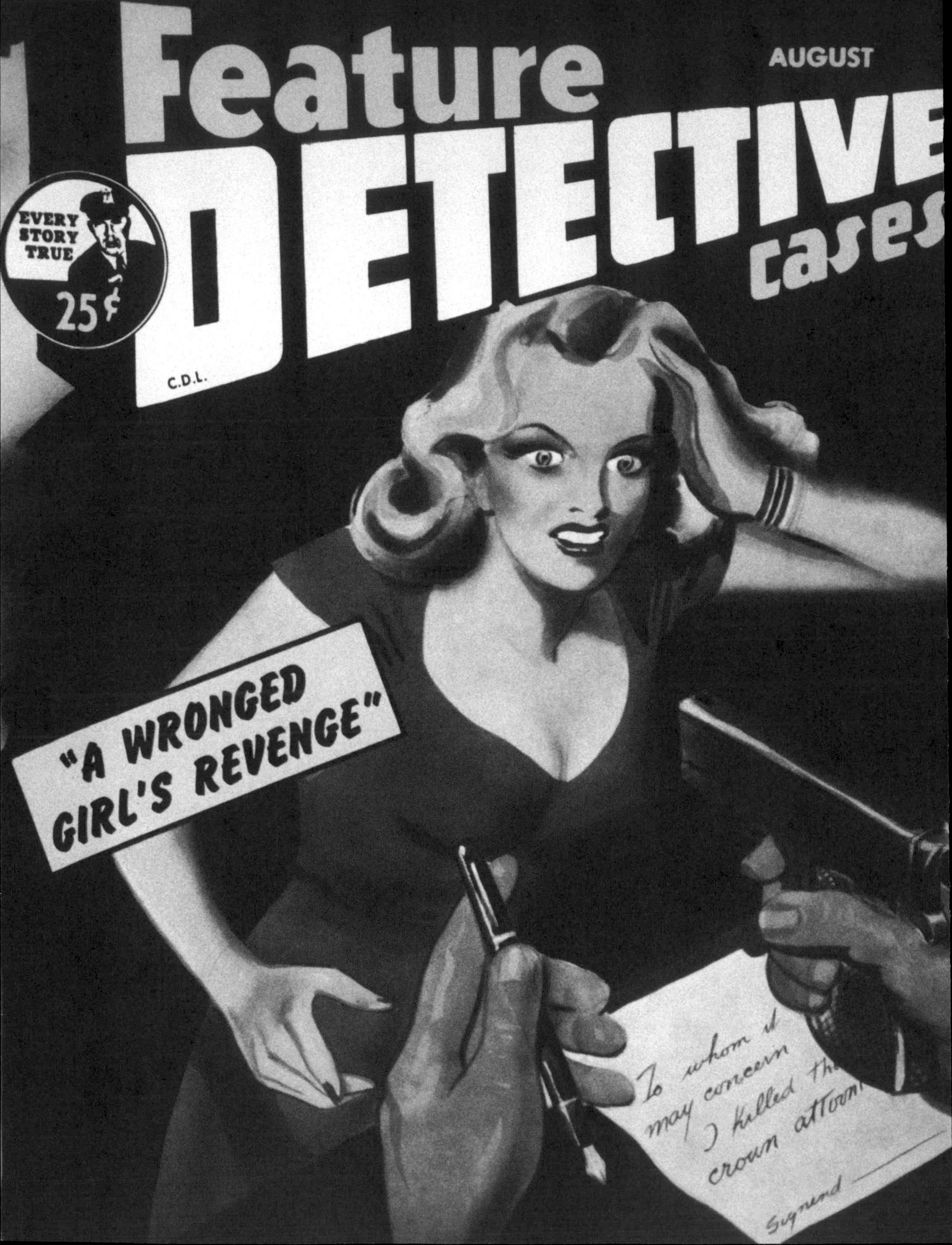

Feature
AUGUST
DETECTIVE
cases
EVERY STORY TRUE
25¢
C.D.L.
"A WRONGED GIRL'S REVENGE"
To whom it may concern
I killed the crown attorn
Signed

Philip Godsell's "Triangle in Scarlet" was typical in attributing emotional intensity to race. It told the story of Charcoal, "a quick-tempered and wiry brave with five wives to his credit." When he arrived home unexpectedly he discovered "his latest and prettiest wife, Wolverine, entertaining Medicine Pipe Stem in a fashion that would make the blood of any husband boil." At the same time, Charcoal was an everyman, a cuckolded husband, but also a "brave" who knew how to handle a rifle and elude the police.

WOMEN WERE VIXENS OR VICTIMS, THE COMPLETELY INNOCENT FEMALE VICTIM BEING A RARITY.

In Tench's "The Love-Crazed Indian," the story starred a typical cast of First Nations people and white lawmen. When a husband and wife were shot on the Anlaw Reserve in northern B.C., neighbours were sure that one of their own, Walter Gungaut, was the culprit. "This Walter … he's woman crazy," one woman reportedly told the B.C. Provincial Police. As insane as the man was alleged to have been, he nonetheless managed to elude his captors thanks to his instinctive bush wits.

Like Charcoal, Gungaut appeared not only as a murderer but as a hold-out against whiteman's law, a common theme in Western novels and movies. Ironically, the dialogue in Tench's story seems to have been lifted from a gangster film: "I've got a gun and lots of shells," Gungaut taunted his captors as they closed in. "If you want me, come and get me, but I'm betting I'll get a few of you first. They can only hang me once, you — cop!" Famous, and fateful, last words. The cops replied by shooting him "stone dead [, a] fitting end for a man who committed double murder for lust."

If "savage love" was typical of First Nations characters in true crime writers' minds, they were equally convinced that people not possessed of Anglo-Protestant fortitude were prone to murderous passions. Without a stiff upper lip it was hard to deal with love's occasional humiliations — like being jilted. When Canada's "foreigners" lashed out, true crime readers discovered, they left "mountains of sorrow and rivers of blood."

John Lycheluk certainly qualified, as described in "Blood Payment for a Love-crazed Fiend." The lovelorn man might have ordered a copy of

53

Making the Honeymoon Last Forever, but neither he nor his intended ever made it to the altar. On the lookout for a wife he looked in the wrong directions, first at his niece, then at his cousin's wife. Publicly humiliated, he struck out not only at the women but their families. In a "fatal night of flame and frenzy," the Prairie farmer set fire to two houses, leaving eight bodies in his murderous wake. Justice was served in this case when the man took his life in prison, saving the state the expense of a trial but robbing the authorities of a trial in which the culprit could be condemned.

A French-Canadian lumberjack was also easily stereotyped in C. V. Tench's story about a married woman killed by her overly amorous lover. Visiting Montreal in 1948, on a trip from the Quebec bush, "swarthy-skinned" Raoul "Frenchy" Bazinet met his amour, Noella Denommée, whom he tried to persuade to marry him. There was one obstacle: the fact that the attractive waitress was already married. Bazinet persisted, pressing her to accept his proposal even after his intended had slapped him in the face in public. Quoting from the police interview, Tench used Bazinet's confession to indict the lovelorn lumberjack: "We had been going together a long time but she wouldn't marry me." When he suggested they repair to a furnished room to talk, he proposed again and she refused again. "I asked her why but she wouldn't answer me," Bazinet continued. "I was mad." Mad enough, Tench concluded wryly, to "bludgeon and strangle the woman whom he professedly loved."

Once in a while, Canadian true crime magazines published stories that purported to show how domestic disasters could push otherwise composed Anglo men to murder. In stories such as "The Case of the Granby Skeleton," the husband's violence was attributed to the victim's failures as a wife. However happy the Herberts may have been when their relationship began, neighbours reported that the couple had fought "like cats and dogs." Phyllis Herbert, like Noella Denommée, slapped her man on the face. Their boarding housekeeper thought it odd that Clarence Herbert rarely hit her back: "'I often wondered why. The woman had such a nasty temper.'" Unwilling or unable to counter his wife's behaviour with a little violence, the humiliated husband hatched a plan to rid himself of her. His first scheme was to commit her to a mental asylum. When the fights persisted after her release he took her from Guelph, Ontario, to Granby, Quebec, where he admitted to police that he had choked her, burned the body and buried it in the woods. But not before removing his wife's wedding ring.

For *True Police Cases* writer Jack Barnes, this band of gold was just one more clue in the interprovincial murder trail brilliantly tracked by "crack

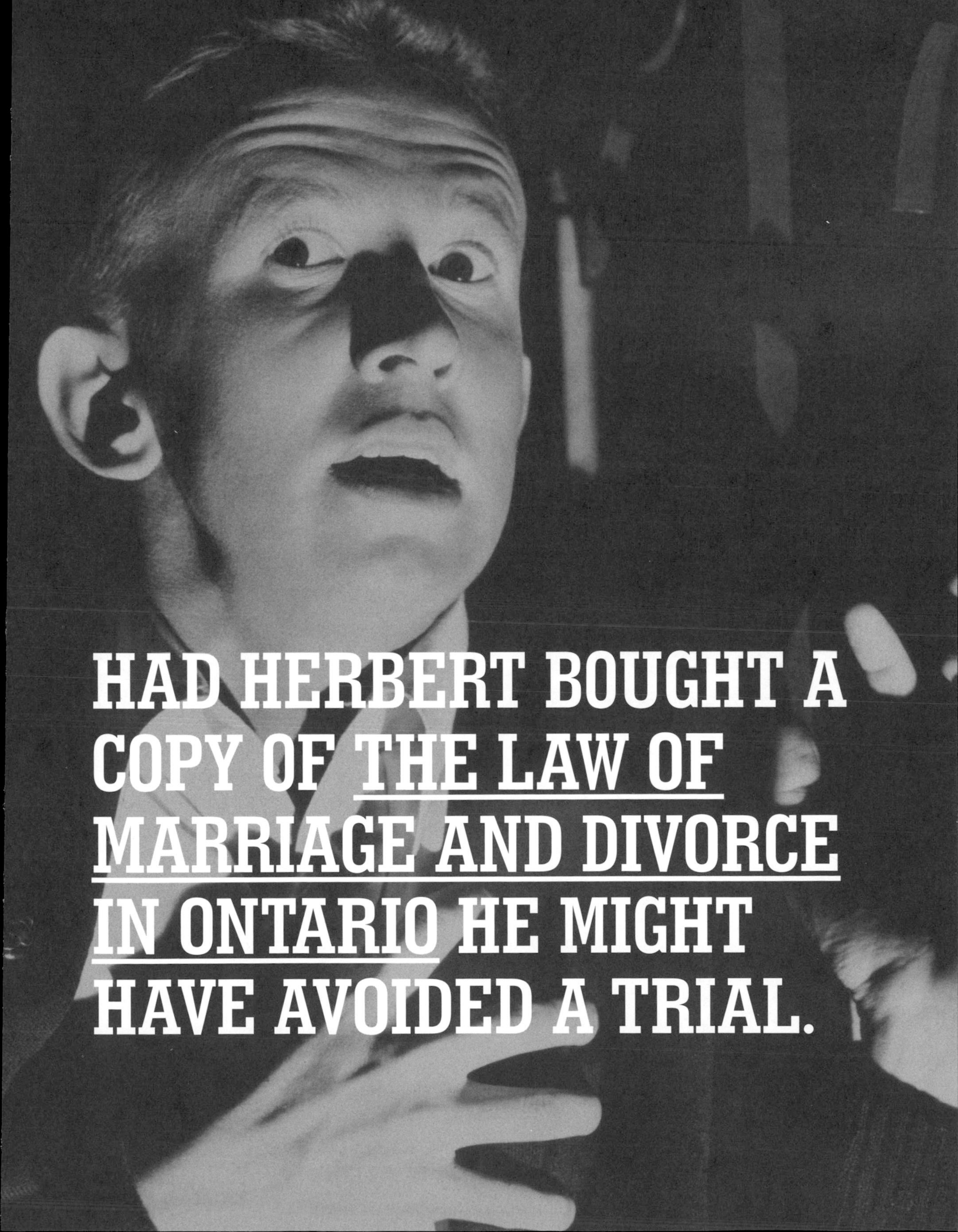
HAD HERBERT BOUGHT A COPY OF THE LAW OF MARRIAGE AND DIVORCE IN ONTARIO HE MIGHT HAVE AVOIDED A TRIAL.

criminologist" Inspector Pinard in 1939. But why had Herbert kept it? As a keepsake? As an offering for another woman? As a piece of jewellery to pawn? Barnes didn't speculate. Herbert's peers were inclined to take a generous view of his actions, however. In the face of considerable evidence that he had planned his wife's murder and made elaborate efforts to cover his tracks, the jury found him guilty of manslaughter, not murder. Had Herbert bought a copy of *The Law of Marriage and Divorce in Ontario* (a manual advertised regularly in the Canadian pulps) he might have avoided a trial. Nevertheless, the evidence of his domestic troubles saved him from the gallows.

SOLD ONLY TO ENGAGED OR MARRIED ADULTS
In an era when the publication of information about birth control was technically illegal, true crime pulps played an important role in providing easy access to the facts of life. Canadians could inform themselves by purchasing books that left no doubt as to their content. Manuals like Sex, Marriage and Birth Control would arrive in a discrete "brown paper wrapper."

Married Love
By Dr. Marie Stopes
(Famous Authority on Sexual Relations)
A book written by an expert, designed to make the marriage concourse a happy, healthful part of sensible living. Sold only to engaged or married adults. Please give age with order.
Shipped Prepaid $2.49
ALEXANDER SALES COMPANY
68 King Street, East
Suite 306
TORONTO, ONTARIO, CANADA

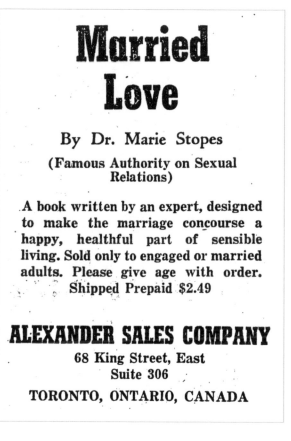

THE UNWRITTEN LAW

Although Canadian true crime magazines were overwhelmingly pro-police, and downright romantic when it came to chronicling the Mounties' law enforcement skills, the purveyors of true crime understood that cultural laws played a role in justice, as well. Particularly when cases involved crimes of the heart. The unwritten law (the unofficial understanding that men were obliged to use violence to protect women's chastity or to avenge threats to their marriages) could reduce a charge from murder to manslaughter and occasionally it could let a killer off the hook. There was no official recognition of this practice in Canadian law, writer James Curtis observed, yet "the courts still lean over backwards in extenuating such crimes of passion."

Wronged men were sympathetic fellows, as the tale "Stratford's Unwritten Law" confirmed. These sorts of killers were ordinary fellows, just like James Crawford, whose "buxom wife Cora" and her "shenanigans" with neighbour Amber Carter drove him to murder. When the St. Mary's, Ontario, couple took in Carter after the man's farmhouse had burned down, the "contemptible ingrate" repaid the favour by making "goo-goo eyes" at Cora. Crawford at first tried to woo back his wife. But when he found Carter "making passionate love to his wife and cooing sweet blandishments in her ear"

ONLY A "SUPINE HUSBAND" WOULD HAVE ALLOWED HIS WIFE TO "DISH ... HIM HUGE DOSES OF THE ROMANTIC DOUBLE CROSS."

FACTUAL
DETECTIVE
STORIES
and DARING
JANUARY
15¢
I GAVE MY LIFE to Crime
Mystery of the
THIRTEEN MURDERED MEN
TRUE CRIME CASES
MURDER IN SWING TIME

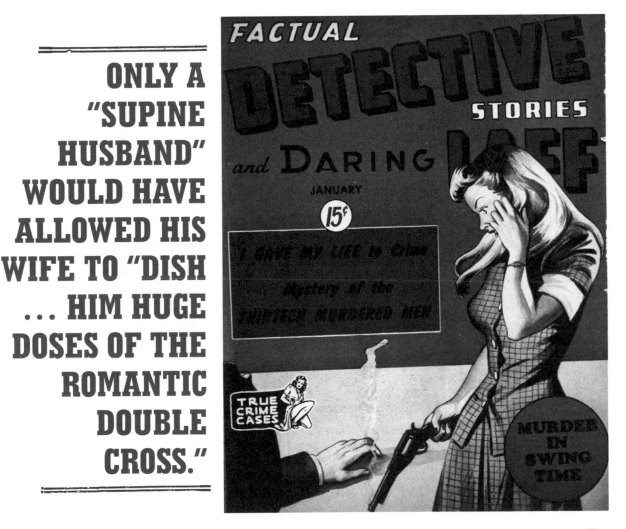

he was driven to desperation.

Only a "supine husband" would have allowed his wife to "dish ... him huge doses of the romantic double cross," according to Curtis, writing in *True Police Cases*. But Crawford reasserted his conjugal authority, like a real man if not a law-abiding citizen, by shooting "the barnyard Lothario" as he walked up his driveway.

Although the shooting had evidently been premeditated, and although the trial judge reminded the jury at Crawford's 1940 trial that "the 'unwritten law' has no place in Canada," Crawford dodged a murder conviction. The jury's verdict of manslaughter seemed appropriate: a temptress and a Lothario could drive even the most level-headed and long-suffering husband to kill. The story concluded with the judge's sentencing statement: "'No doubt your lot has been a hard one, and we sympathize with you. However you took the law into your own hands when you might have obtained redress under the law.'" Fourteen years in Kingston seemed to satisfy both the judge and the case chronicler.

While this she-had-it-coming genre of love-gone-wrong stories usually featured cuckolded husbands out for revenge, there were variations on the theme. In 19th-century melodramas and popular Westerns the damsel in distress sometimes found herself without a male protector. Women like this could take the law into their own hands and many people, including jury members, agreed, even if such actions technically violated the law.

A classic story of an unlikely heroine's self-vindication and legal exoneration was "The Case of Clara Ford." Published in a 1943 issue of *Daring Crime* (lifted verbatim from a 1931 book, *Murders and Mysteries in Canada*) almost 50 years after Ford's trial, it recounted how the woman, disguised in men's clothes, had shot Frank Westwood and got away with it. As author "Mac Burton" (actually W. Stewart Wallace) reflected, "It is not often that a prisoner accused of murder confesses to the commission of the crime, and actually pleads guilty in court, and yet is after trial triumphantly acquitted and allowed to go free."

On the one hand Ford, a "mulatto" seamstress who lived in the "coloured" quarter of downtown Toronto, was a believable killer (the woman had previously lived near Westwood, she owned a gun, she sported men's attire); on the other, her confessed motive — that young Westwood had indecently assaulted her — improbably cast her respectable white victim as a rake. Crown witnesses contradicted this characterization, suggesting that Ford was actually smitten with Westwood, who rebuffed her. Taking the stand in her own defence, Ford presented yet another story, claiming that big-city detectives had manipulated her into confessing. "This does the boys of Toronto credit," she crowed after the gentlemen of the jury acquitted her.

DOING RIGHT BY WRONGED LOVERS

The true crime pulps were a moralizing medium. But of all the sorts of cases published in the magazines, the broken-hearted people who resorted to violence out of anger or despair were the most understandable sorts of criminals. If they were members of ethnic groups stereotyped as inordinately passionate, or beyond the pale of civilization, then their actions could be attributed to their fixed racial characteristics, their bad choice of partners or their misuse of alcohol.

In contrast the pulps often painted mate killers who were otherwise upstanding citizens, and who traced their origins to Britain, as ordinary people who snapped under extraordinary emotional pressure. The Anglo men who wrote for the pulps seem to have identified with these killers and they invited readers to put themselves into the shoes of men whose wives had slapped them in the face, whether literally or metaphorically. As the story of the "Lothario" murder opened: "What would you do in the case of a man who … was invited to sleep under your roof, eat and drink from your table, wear your clothes and then — try to steal your wife?"

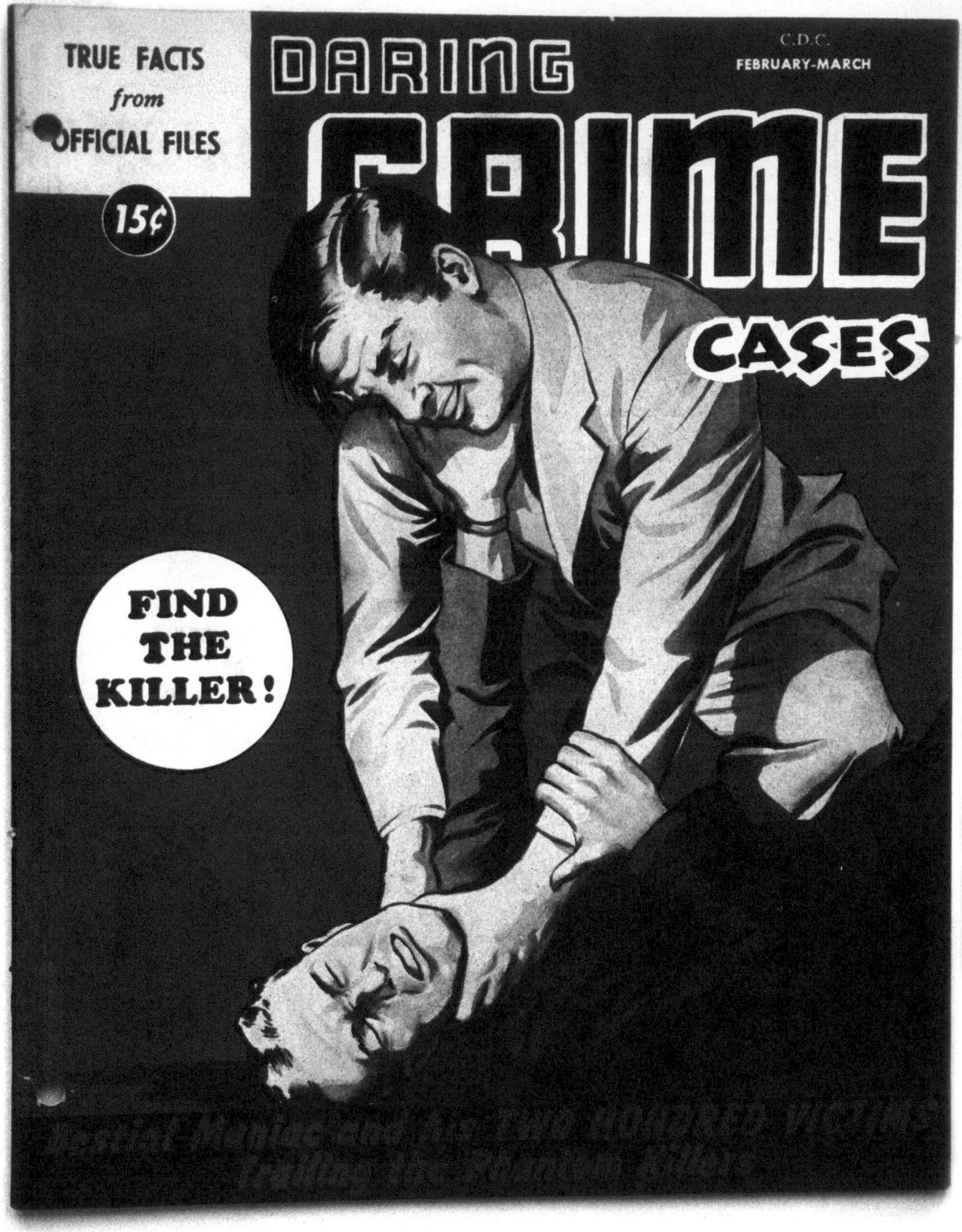
TRUE FACTS
from
OFFICIAL FILES
15¢
DARING
CRIME
CASES
C.D.C.
FEBRUARY-MARCH
FIND THE KILLER!

4

DEATH FOR GAIN

"THOU SHALT NOT COVET THY NEIGHBOUR'S OX." That might have registered with the ancients but it didn't sink into the heads of the men, and the few women, who decided to help themselves to other people's belongings. Cash, jewellery, booze and cars were the prime temptations in modern Canada, and the pulps published stories about people who were desperate enough, daring enough and mean enough to kill for goods they coveted.

Stories involving death for gain were the true crime pulps' bread and butter. They were well-suited to the police procedural genre because thieves went after items that brainy cops could trace, whether they were fur pelts nabbed on the northern frontier or knick-knacks swiped from a city store. Professional thieves could be collared when they tried to fence stolen goods; amateurs were easier catches, because they kept incriminating evidence close at hand. Even cash was traceable, particularly if down-and-outers suddenly pulled out rolls of bills and splashed money around. Police officers frequently caught crooks red-handed, wearing their victim's jewellery or sporting dead men's clothes. And then there was the rat — the resentful gang member who hadn't got his share, or the moll willing to squeal on her fella if he didn't deliver on his promises.

Unlike crimes motivated by lust or revenge, robbery and burglary were invariably premeditated, sometimes planned well in advance. This was especially true in stories involving gangs of thieves, from the glamorous train robbers of the early railroad era to the safe-cracking pros of the Depression.

Few of these criminals had intended to kill when they set about to rob, and some hadn't even carried weapons to the scenes of their crimes. Nonetheless, the pulps showed how easily greed could lead to murder, whether it meant killing a plucky storekeeper or a cringing pensioner, or silencing a potential witness. According to pulp writers, these heists gone wrong spelled the beginning of the end for crooks and bandits who had managed for a time to live off the proceeds of crime.

In an era not far removed from the Depression, then beset by war sacrifices, pulp writers were drawn to cases involving criminals who had fancied that hard cash could be had without hard work. This was not a peculiarly Canadian value, but few Canadians in this period questioned the connection between honest work and respectability. Indeed, during the 1930s thousands of men and women had marched and protested for the right to earn an honest day's wage. Perhaps this is why the true crime pulps published so many stories about humble folk who ought to have known the moral worth of a day's work but took what they figured was the easy road to fortune, albeit one that led to death. Rather than retell the stories of crafty cat burglars and oily charmers (the sorts who populated highbrow hardback collections), the pulps featured "would-be big shots" who had reckoned they could steal and cheat their way out of poverty. True crime writers set the record straight: the once cocky crook's downfall and his humiliation before the law was inevitable.

NO HONOUR AMONG THIEVES

There was nothing new about men getting together to rob and steal. Dickens had made a name for himself by leading respectable readers into England's urban underworld, where thieves petty and powerful operated. North American dime novels dramatized the depredations of criminal gangs in new cities as well as on the lawless frontier. Once the movies became popular in the early 20th century, cops-and-robbers flicks vied with cowboys-and-Indians pictures for popularity.

True crime magazines showed that truth was every bit as dramatic as fiction when it came to the exploits of organized gangs. Train bandits and bank robbers gave city cops and the men of the mounted a run for their money. They were bold enough and practised enough to live off the proceeds of crime, but lawmen invariably tracked them down because there was no honour among thieves.

When the Canadian Pacific Railway finally snaked its way across

Canada in 1885 it opened up commerce as well as mountain passes. In the Far West, through the Rockies, trains had to chug slowly up steep grades, affording passengers scenic views and providing prime picking grounds for thieves. Trains were rolling banks, loaded with cash, registered mail, gold bullion and silver ingots — quite a temptation for ambitious thieves. While it was possible for one person to pickpocket from passengers, it took a few men to hold up an express train. Some, like Bill Miner's gang, did it with style. Still famous four decades after their 1904 holdup of a gold-laden train near Mission, British Columbia, the gang inspired a true crime story that cast Miner as the last of the old west outlaws and a throwback to Robin Hood: "To the poorer folks he was a god. He gave them money and befriended them. Though willing to use the friendship of men and women in high places, he had nothing but contempt for their station. The poor people were his people."

Old-time thieves like Miner, whose "mis-spent life" had morally redeeming qualities, were apparently figures of the past. In pulp stories about modern-day heists, gangs were considerably less polished, less honourable and more likely to be "foreigners." The case of "the Crow's Nest Hold-Up," committed in 1920, continued to generate true crime stories in the 1940s. It had everything: a robbery scheme, a bold stickup, a posse chase, a shootout with the police and, of course, an execution.

The story began with three bandits' "miscarried plans" to carry out a robbery, not of a train but of one of its passengers: bootlegger Emilio Picariello. Known to carry wads of money, "Emperor Pic" regularly rode the train from Lethbridge, Alberta to Fernie, B.C., conducting his business of supplying "bootleg liquor to quench the thirst of the miners who frequented the brothels, wide-open bars and gambling hells he operated on the Alberta side of the Crow's Nest Pass." Here was a case of thieves preying on thieves. The bandit trio's plans went awry, however, when the "cunning bootleg king" slipped out at Blairmore, Alberta, while the men were playing poker. Frustrated that "Pic" had eluded them, the gang held up passengers at gunpoint, netting "a paltry four hundred dollars, and a handful of watches, rings and trinkets."

On the lam and chased by posses, Tom Bassoff and his "Russian-born" compatriots, Ausby Auloff and a man by the name of Ackroff, made their way through "wild rocky country" to the small town of Bellevue, Alberta. As the police closed in on them at the Bellevue Café they didn't lay down their arms, as Miner's gang had done, but blasted their way out, killing one officer and wounding another in a fierce gun battle. Bassoff and Auloff were injured, too, but as Bassoff staggered out of the café he stopped and shot his wounded partner in the head. When the dust cleared and officers examined the dead man's body, they found only a single dollar in his pockets. Apparently the third man, Ackroff, had made away with the loot and robbed his fellow thieves of their share. Dishonour and double-crossing had led the greedy

DARE-DEVIL
DETECTIVE
STORIES
JANUARY, 1942
15 CENTS
DARE-DEVIL DETECTIVE

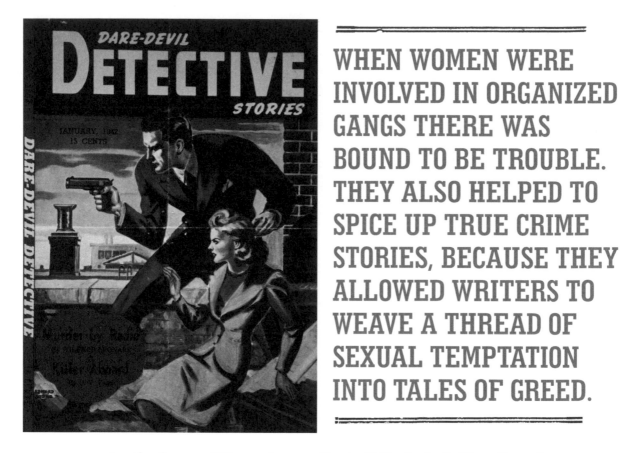

WHEN WOMEN WERE INVOLVED IN ORGANIZED GANGS THERE WAS BOUND TO BE TROUBLE. THEY ALSO HELPED TO SPICE UP TRUE CRIME STORIES, BECAUSE THEY ALLOWED WRITERS TO WEAVE A THREAD OF SEXUAL TEMPTATION INTO TALES OF GREED.

gang leader to a fitting end, according to Philip Godsell: "Tom Bassoff, unregenerate and defiant, mounted the scaffold in the snow-swept courtyard and with a snarl still on his lips plunged downward to his doom."

Thieves who resorted to violence in the course of committing robberies were guilty not only of murder but of violating the work ethic, a prominent moral theme in the true crime pulps and a favourite theme of writer Godsell. He seemed to look for cases that showed how crooks, who figured they could make money without working, were also willing to cheat their fellow gang members to keep their goods or save their own necks. "Blood on the Christmas Snow," a story about a gang that preyed upon hard-working gold prospectors (on Christmas Day, no less) provided a perfect illustration. The plan was ruthless from the start. When George O'Brien met a man by the name of Graves in jail in Dawson, he tempted his fellow prisoner with a surefire way to make a pile of easy money: "Why not camp at some lonely spot along the trail, keep a lookout for gold-burdened miners mushing south, throw a gun on them, take their gold and notes and shove their bodies through the ice?"

Feature
MAY
EVERY STORY TRUE
25¢
DETECTIVE
cases
C.D.L.
Sensational!
WOMEN
IN
CRIME
Daring!
NOT FIT TO BE
A MOTHER

Following through on O'Brien's plans, the pair ambushed three miners making their way back south from the Yukon's goldfields on Christmas Day, 1901, killing each of them and submerging their bodies under the ice. O'Brien was arrested with more than $2,000 hidden amongst his goods — a suspiciously large amount for a man who appeared not to work. But his fate was sealed when a second man, whom O'Brien had approached while imprisoned, ratted on the triple murderer. The prisoner, an American cardsharp known as "The Clear Kid," testified that O'Brien had let him in on his scheme "to clean up a bunch o' coin an' chuck their bodies in the drink." O'Brien had already done his share of double-crossing, however. Several weeks after his execution the bullet-riddled body of his erstwhile partner, Graves, washed up on a sandbar in the Yukon River.

When women were involved in organized gangs there was bound to be trouble. They also helped to spice up true crime stories, because they allowed writers to weave a thread of sexual temptation into tales of greed. Their depictions of gals who consorted with professional thieves bore a striking resemblance to the images of brazen-faced women on pulp magazine covers. Women like Rosella Gorovenko, found in a Vancouver flophouse bed with not one but two suspected killers, were willing to rat on their fellow thieves, especially if one was a welshing fiancé.

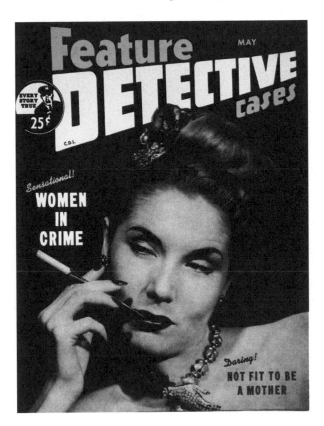

W. W. Bride gave Gorovenko a starring role as a villainess. Although an accomplice in a robbery that had led to "the merciless killing of a [Japanese] Vancouver shopkeeper," the "attractive dark-eyed little damsel" testified for the Crown, explaining how the men had "cased the joints they were going to take," loaded up with liquor, "hoisted" a car and proceeded on a "campaign of crime that was to end in robbery and death." A graduate of a juvenile detention home, Gorovenko knew her way around the law. When asked if she had offered testimony in exchange for leniency, she aimed for the moral high road: "I decided these Japanese had as much right to live as anyone else" — a remarkable statement, considering Canadians' animosity toward the Japanese in the wake of the attack on Pearl Harbor.

After her testimony convicted her ex-boyfriends along with two of their mates, one of the men, an active serviceman, expressed far less honourable sentiments toward the victim: "I hope you guys feel happy and good because you want to string up four boys for one lousy Jap." Luckily for them, the British Columbia Court of Appeal agreed, rendering its verdict just as the internment of the province's Japanese population was under way.

In the case written up as "The Winnipeg Diamond Mystery," a moll proved even craftier than Gorovenko when it came to finding a man with money and several other men to bump him off. Annie Selbach had informed the police that she had merely worked as a nursemaid and housekeeper for John Penny, a man who had been bludgeoned to death with a claw hammer. Under questioning, Selbach admitted that Penny had favoured her in his will. Working with the theory that Selbach had promised to split the legacy with the man who could hasten her employer's death, Winnipeg police discovered that she had managed to tempt four men "well known for their weakness for women." As writer Jack Truscott told it, "a girl as attractive as Annie, coupled to the money she was expected to receive upon the death of John Penny, would offer tempting bait for them."

But Annie Selbach, like Rosella Gorovenko, traded incriminating evidence for leniency, pinning the blame for the murder on the one man who had escaped. When John Stanton was finally captured he admitted that he had been in on the plan to "go after the old man's diamonds, even if they had to croak the old guy." But he insisted that one of the other men had actually done the killing. Betrayed by a conniving temptress and a rat, he "forced a smile" and faced his fate like a man.

THE "GREAT DATE" BLOUSE

If clothes made the man, moulded latex made the woman, rendering her fit to fill out Elizabeth of Hollywood's "original creation." This ad for a "lovely 'dress-up' blouse of silky luxury rayon in figure-flattering design" made an appeal to women readers to try out this garment that was "trimmed in the finest imported lace."

ELIZABETH OF HOLLYWOOD • ELIZABETH OF HOLLYWOOD • ELIZABETH

EXCLUSIVE!

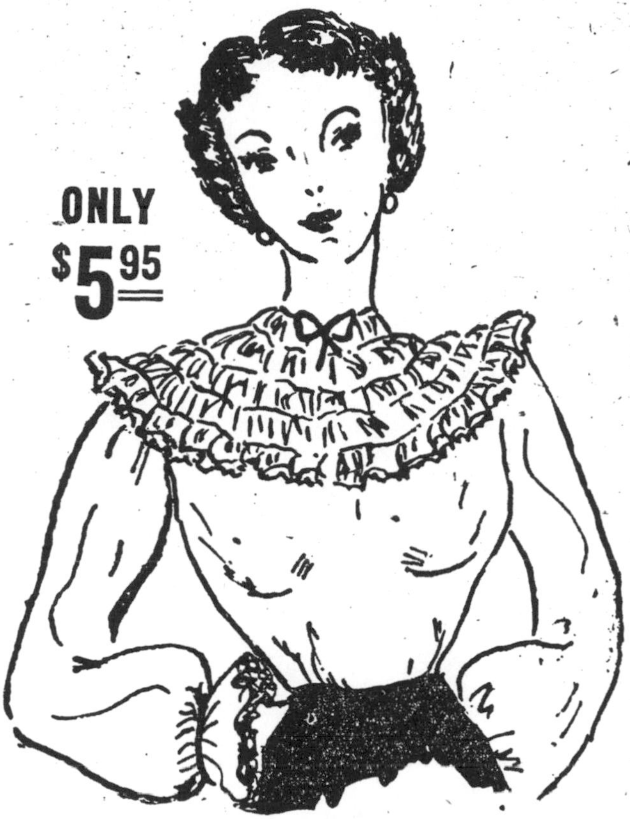

ONLY $5.95

Elizabeth of HOLLYWOOD presents An Original Creation "GREAT DATE" BLOUSE

From Fashion's "Main Stem," Elizabeth of Hollywood creates for YOU a lovely "dress-up" blouse of silky luxury rayon in figure-flattering design . . . You'll love the full-length, adjustable sleeves, designed to be worn at any length. You'll thrill to the fragile beauty of the frilly, gathered yoke, trimmed in finest imported lace. It's a serviceable, dressy blouse, too, for year-round smartness.

Elizabeth of Hollywood designers' superb workmanship guarantees the highest quality.

The "Great Date" blouse, for thrilling Saturday night chic, is available exclusively by mail in perfect sizes, 14 to 20. This lovely blouse comes in two shades—Pure White and Pale Blue.

REMEMBER: An exclusive arrangement with Elizabeth of Hollywood brings these original, exclusive fashions to Canada BY MAIL ONLY.

That's why it's an Elizabeth of Hollywood Exclusive!

EXAMINE IT AT OUR EXPENSE!
IF NOT DELIGHTED,
RETURN WITHIN 5 DAYS AND
YOUR MONEY WILL BE REFUNDED

Read What Others Say!

Writes Wm. Brown-Forbes, President of Cinevision:

"Elizabeth of Hollywood has always been costumier for all my motion pictures and television shows. If a garment bears the stamp of her genius, it's tops in fashion and quality!"

And

Arlene Janssen, famous model, says:

". . . Delightful, the prettiest blouse I've ever worn! It's just adorable! Please design my wedding gown and use this letter if you wish! All your designs have so much chic!"

For Men Only!

And you males, who don't know rep from satin, this advertisement is for you, too. Send today for one of these Elizabeth of Hollywood blouses for sweetheart, wife, mother or sister . . . for birthdays, anniversaries or Christmas . . . or just to show good taste. They'll love you for it! The "Great Date" blouse comes tissue-wrapped and stylishly boxed.

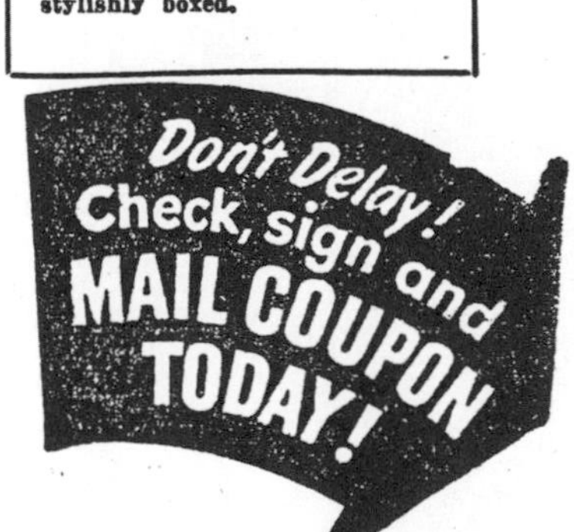
Don't Delay!
Check, sign and
MAIL COUPON
TODAY!

ALEXANDER SALES CO.,
P.O. Box 43, Station K, Toronto, Ont.

Send me a lovely "Great Date" blouse made to measure by Elizabeth of Hollywood. My size is .... and I prefer .... color.

( ) I enclose $5.95, send blouse postpaid.
( ) Send C.O.D. I'll pay postman $5.95 plus postage and C.O.D. charges.

NAME ....

ADDRESS ....

....

ELIZABETH OF HOLLYWOOD • ELIZABETH OF HOLLYWOOD • ELIZABETH

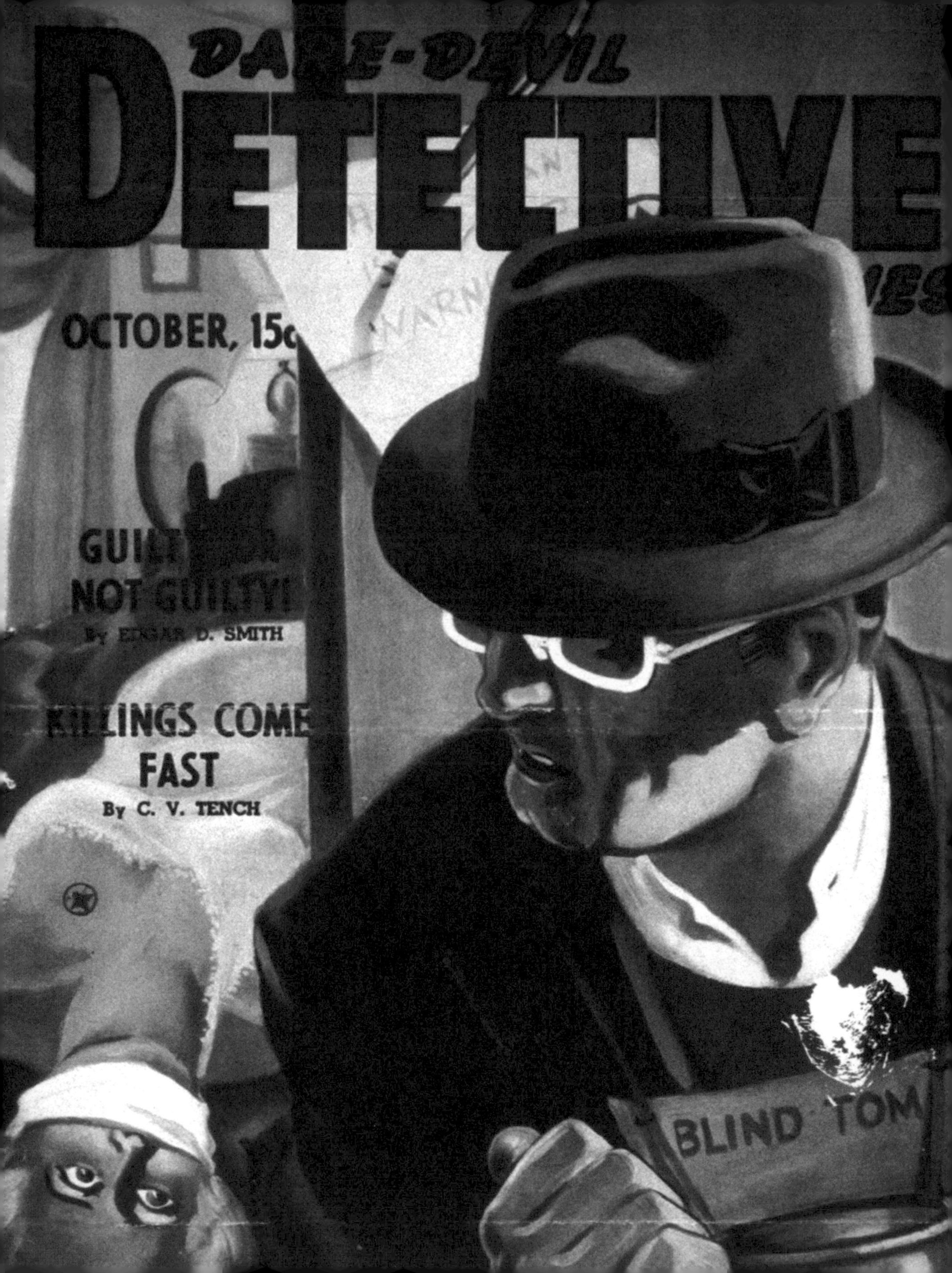
DARE-DEVIL
DETECTIVE
OCTOBER, 15c
NOT GUILTY!
KILLINGS COME
FAST
By C. V. TENCH
BLIND TOM

CANADA'S MEANEST KILLERS

Knocking off people with stashes of diamonds or pocketsful of gold nuggets was one thing, but robbing from the poor and defenceless merited the sternest moral commentary in the true crime pulps. These were not crimes committed by professional thieves but by men who lashed out when they discovered that their victims had fewer valuables or less cash than they had hoped to steal. If true crime writers could eke out a measure of sympathy for robbers betrayed by their molls and their mates, they showed no mercy when they turned to cases of cold-hearted killers.

In stories such as "The Clue of the Chinese Bowl," the robber's cruelty always turned on the victim's virtue. The contrast between "badly crippled and arthritic" Alice Chapman, a "cheerful octogenarian," and the man convicted of her murder, a small-time peddler and bootlegger named Walter Zablotny, could not have been stronger. Mrs. Chapman's "indomitable spirit naturally won the admiration of the people in [Port Credit]," W. W. Bride opened his story. In spite of her afflictions she had opened her little store daily, supplying the neighbourhood with small goods. Zablotny lived in a shack near a train yard: "He was not a worker but he always seemed to have a little money." The Toronto Township Police suspected that he might have been

THE TORONTO TOWNSHIP POLICE SUSPECTED THAT HE MIGHT HAVE BEEN THE "FIEND" WHO BROKE INTO MRS. CHAPMAN'S STORE, RANSACKED IT AND STABBED THE "POOR SOUL" IN THE FACE WITH A SCREWDRIVER.

the "fiend" who broke into Mrs. Chapman's store, ransacked it and stabbed the "poor soul" in the face with a screwdriver. The case proved difficult to crack until some of the items missing from the store (including the Chinese bowl) turned up in Zablotny's wife's possession. The suspect's damning generosity toward his family provided another clue. The victim had kept old

69

$1 bills on a shelf; a bank clerk reported that Zablotny had deposited the same, changing a few dollars for pennies that he presented to his son on his birthday a few days after the murder. Zablotny was convicted on circumstantial evidence alone, but Bride was satisfied that the police had got it right: "The callous killer paid his penalty."

If police traced Zablotny through his dealings with a dead woman's goods, it was arrogance and boastfulness that ultimately led to Rufus Pitre's conviction in Bride's story "New Brunswick's Clueless Crime." There were two victims in this case: South Tatamagouche storekeepers Mr. and Mrs. George Smith. (It appears geography was not a strength for some true crime writers. South Tatamagouche is in Nova Scotia — a fact that makes the title for this story a bit puzzling. The irony is that author, W. W. Bride, was a Vancouver schoolteacher). Like Mrs. Chapman, the Smiths were elderly, hard-working entrepreneurs. Although the stock market crash had hit them hard, they had managed to invest what little remained of their savings in a humble store. Thus, when the Pitre brothers broke in all they found was a bit of tobacco "and a meagre collection of bills and change." Although the "plucky old man" tried to distract the bandits from the cash boxes in the couple's bedroom, they blasted him with a shotgun and proceeded upstairs. W.W. Bride invented the dialogue between the "snarling" killer and the "trembling" woman:

"BETTER GET THAT DOUGH FOR US BEFORE WE GET ROUGH WITH YOU," HE SAID IN A MENACING TONE.

"IT'S ALL WE HAVE," SOBBED THE AGED LADY. "IT'S ALL WE HAVE IN THE WORLD."

Hoping for a bigger haul, the two men made do and melted into the night.

Cash and tobacco are difficult to trace, but not when killers brag about their exploits. A tip from an informant revealed that the brothers Pitre "had been heard to boast that they had recently pulled a job and had come into a tidy sum of money." When the Mounties discovered incriminating evidence (packages of groceries, a box stuffed with small bills) in the Pitres' possession, the younger brother cracked under questioning and explained how his brother Rufus had shot the man during the robbery. Well-defended by a skilled defence lawyer, Rufus Pitre was acquitted. But the case did not end there. A successful Crown appeal led to the elder Pitre's retrial, this time with a new witness who sealed his fate. A prisoner from the Bathurst Jail testified that Rufus Pitre, "confident that he could not be tried a second time for the same offence . . . had bragged of the way in which he had slaughtered the aged storekeeper." As cocky as he was heartless, this killer dug his own grave.

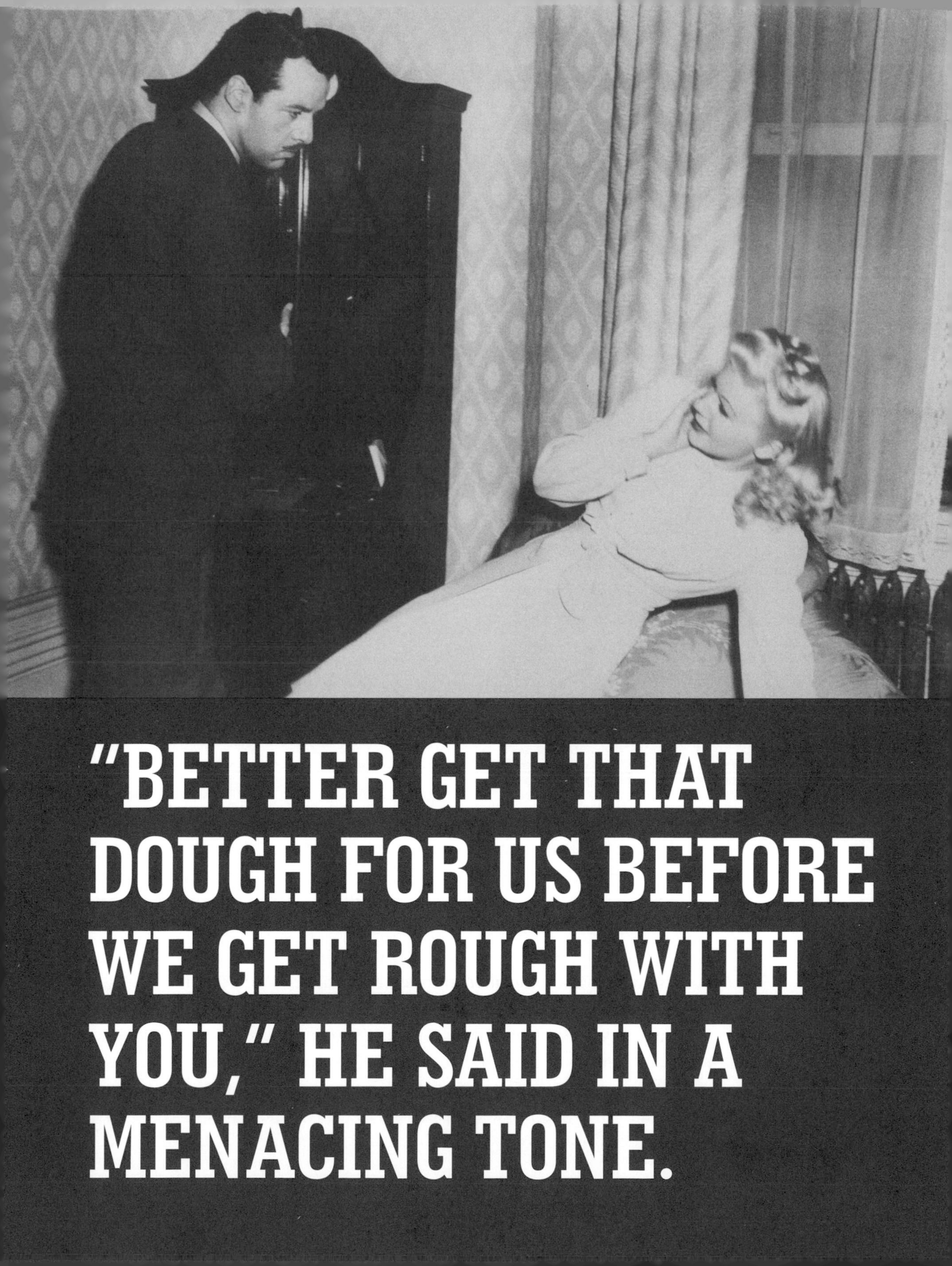

"BETTER GET THAT DOUGH FOR US BEFORE WE GET ROUGH WITH YOU," HE SAID IN A MENACING TONE.

There was little scope for doubt about C. V. Tench's evaluation of a trio of men eventually executed for the murder of Anna Cottick. From the title, "Canada's Three Meanest Killers," Tench provided a convincing case that the men deserved the moniker. Once again, the theme of hard-drinking and out-of-work young men preying on industrious but poor elderly people played out with particular cruelty. This time the setting was a lonely farmhouse on the Manitoba prairie in the midst of the Depression. The stillness of the night was shattered on May 13, 1938, when three men high on homebrew shot their way into the old-age pensioners' modest home. Yanking them out of their beds, they yelled: "'Come on! Tell us where your money's hidden!'," according to Tench. As usual in these cases, the victims' claims that they were poor inspired only rage. The men began "beating and kicking Elko and Anna Cottick savagely and unmercifully in a brutal effort to force them to reveal the hiding place of the money they believed was concealed somewhere on the premises." Tench invited his readers to share his disgust: "Savagely beating and kicking a helpless ninety-one-year-old man and an eighty-one-year-old woman!"

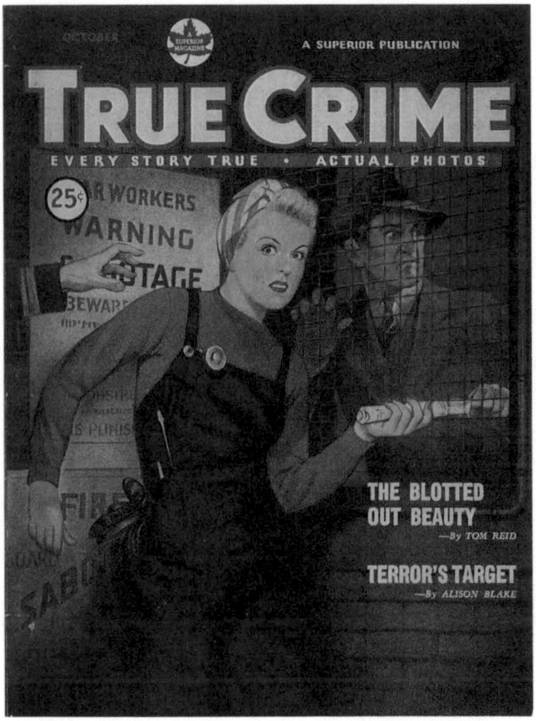
A SUPERIOR PUBLICATION
TRUE CRIME
EVERY STORY TRUE • ACTUAL PHOTOS
25¢
THE BLOTTED OUT BEAUTY
—By TOM REID
TERROR'S TARGET
—By ALISON BLAKE
(Will Straw Collection)

Cracking this case required penetrating the close Ukrainian settlement of Fishing River, 30 miles from Dauphin, Manitoba. The men of the mounted realized that residents were reluctant to talk because they feared reprisals. Tench detailed how this crime was connected to others: "For some time now a wave of terrorism had been sweeping the district. A barn burnt down here, a house there, residents beaten up, petty robberies." And so it was that the police traced a local gang, suspected of these crimes, to the shocking murder. Using a new high-tech tactic — bugging the men's jail cells — combined with the tried-and-true method of grilling the weakest link until he was ready to rat, the Mounties provided enough evidence to convict three local men for the cruel murder, "an end well deserved," Tench concluded, "by Canada's three meanest killers."

THE GLOSS OFF GLAMOUR

Most robberies and thefts with violence provided insufficient narrative material to merit a true crime story. The essential feature was a tricky police chase, but every now and then an arresting character gave a true crime writer so much more to work with. Murder committed in Mafia hits or other

ONCE IN A WHILE, CANADA BRED ITS OWN GLAMOROUS KILLERS, MEN AND WOMEN WHO REVELLED IN THE BRIGHT LIGHTS OF FAME AND FORTUNE BEFORE ENDING THEIR LIVES IN PRISON, ON THE GALLOWS OR IN A HAIL OF BULLETS.

SMASH CRIME STORIES
TRUE POLICE Cases
WANTED
FOR MURDER
MARY SMITH
JULY
25¢
RED RYAN—
Crookdom's Ace Phoney!
CANADA'S
FEMALE PUBLIC ENEMY
TRUE POLICE CASES
25¢

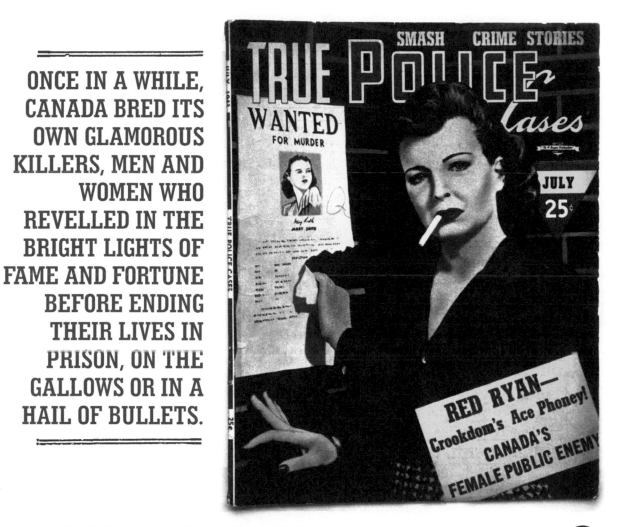

gangland slayings supplied writers of U.S. stories with plenty of colourful personalities to explore. Once in a while, however, Canada bred its own glamorous killers, men and women who revelled in the bright lights of fame and fortune before ending their lives in prison, on the gallows or in a hail of bullets.

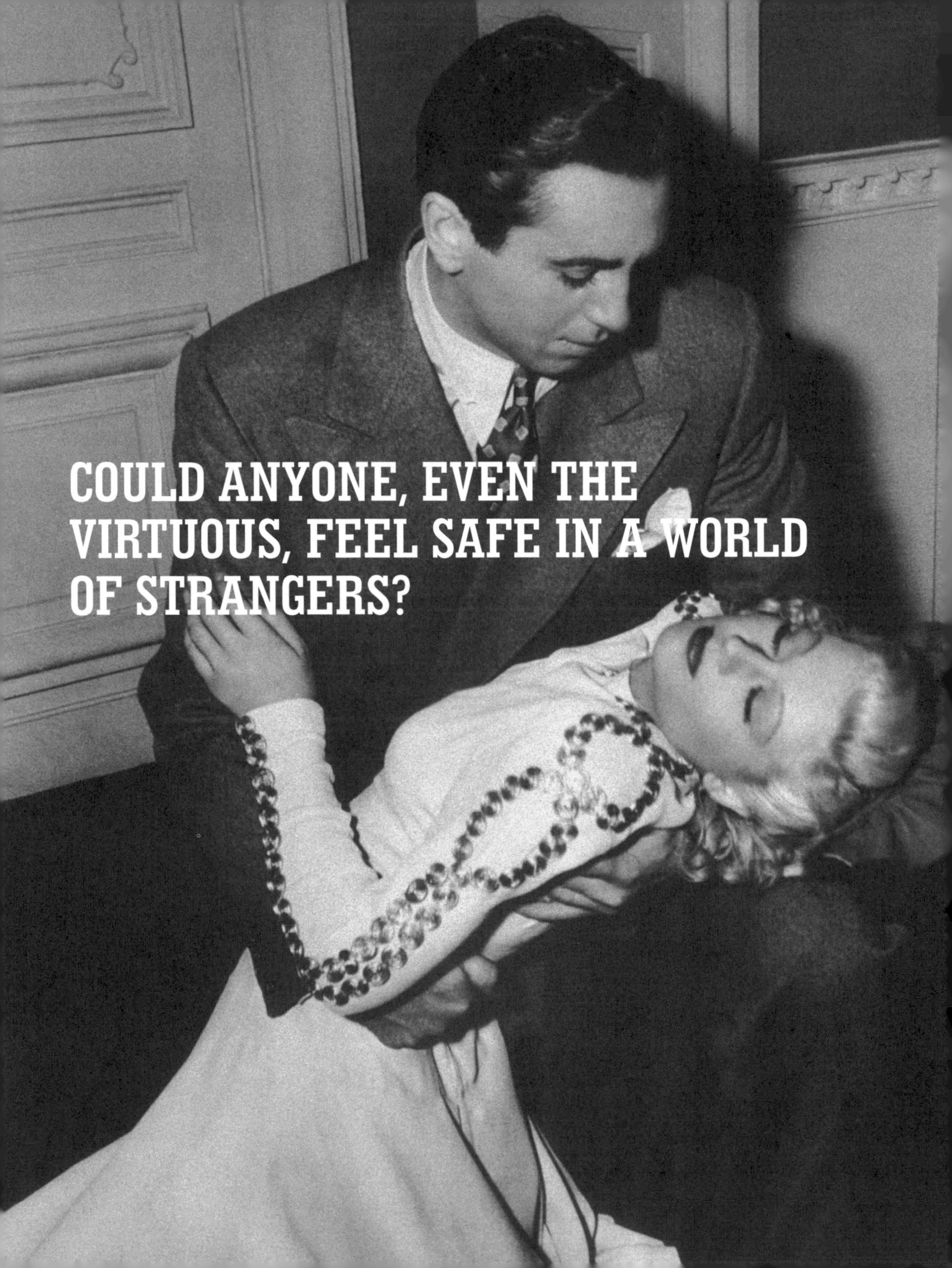

COULD ANYONE, EVEN THE VIRTUOUS, FEEL SAFE IN A WORLD OF STRANGERS?

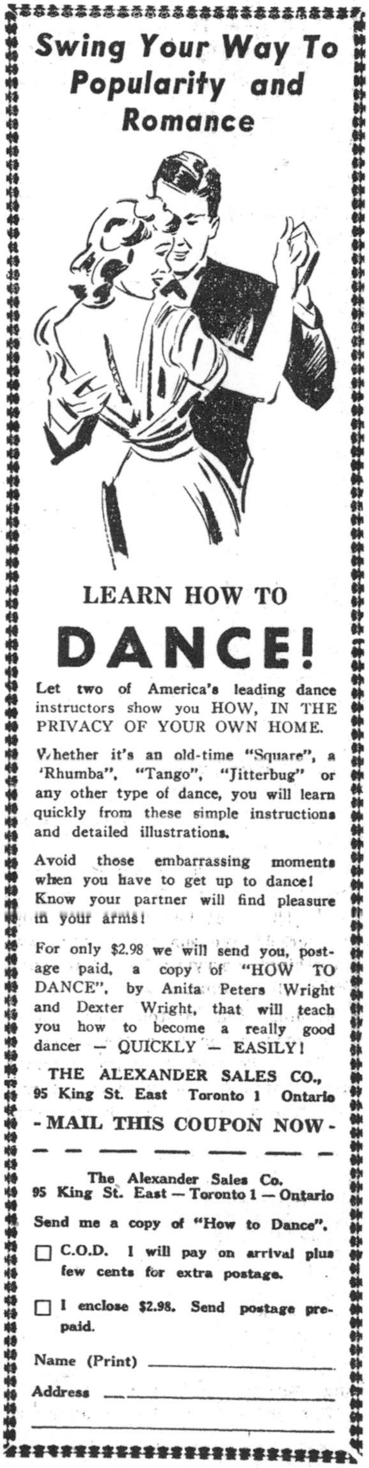
Swing Your Way To Popularity and Romance
LEARN HOW TO
DANCE!
Let two of America's leading dance instructors show you HOW, IN THE PRIVACY OF YOUR OWN HOME.
Whether it's an old-time "Square", a 'Rhumba", "Tango", "Jitterbug" or any other type of dance, you will learn quickly from these simple instructions and detailed illustrations.
Avoid those embarrassing moments when you have to get up to dance! Know your partner will find pleasure in your arms!
For only $2.98 we will send you, postage paid, a copy of "HOW TO DANCE", by Anita Peters Wright and Dexter Wright, that will teach you how to become a really good dancer — QUICKLY — EASILY!
THE ALEXANDER SALES CO., 95 King St. East Toronto 1 Ontario
- MAIL THIS COUPON NOW -
The Alexander Sales Co. 95 King St. East — Toronto 1 — Ontario
Send me a copy of "How to Dance".
C.O.D. I will pay on arrival plus few cents for extra postage.
I enclose $2.98. Send postage prepaid.
Name (Print)
Address

Canada's answer to Bonnie and Clyde, Doris and George MacDonald inspired several pulp writers. Twenty years after their Roaring Twenties crime spree, the pair's tale continued to provide good magazine copy. The MacDonalds, he from Nova Scotia and she from New York state, along with an American accomplice, were already experienced "paperhangers" and "swindle artists" when they rolled into Montreal in 1927 for a spate of "hitting it up on the bubbly." Passing themselves off as a wedding party, the "smartly dressed man" and the "extraordinarily beautiful blonde" registered under aliases in an expensive suite at the sumptuous Mount Royal Hotel, racking up a $160 booze bill. Set on extending their bender, they hatched a plan to hire a taxi driver whom they intended to rob. Whether or not they had planned to kill Adelard Bouchard, the cabbie was shot to death during the trip and relieved of $300 in cash. Had Doris not shed at the murder scene "a small and expensive pair of women's shoes, fine silk hose, lace trimmed underthings and a light silk summer dress, all streaked and stained with blood," the crime might never have been traced to the MacDonalds.

In Godsell's version of their story it was this insatiable love of finery, combined with their distaste for honest labour, that led to the couple's capture. Leaving a "trail of bad and unpaid bills" in their wake, the MacDonalds had snaked their way through the U.S. in the aftermath of "Montreal's Honeymoon Slaying." When American detectives eventually caught up with the pair they provided evidence of their colourful background. Godsell recounted the evidence about the "headstrong" Doris and the "hypnotic" George:

TOGETHER THEY'D TOURED THE STATES IN STOLEN CARS, MAKING THEIR WAY WITH SMALL TIME ROBBERIES, HOLD-UPS, AND WHATEVER MEANS HAPPENED TO PRESENT THEMSELVES OF ACQUIRING EASY MONEY.

Like all thieves they preferred not to work for money. In Doris' case, she had turned to crime only after she had discovered she didn't have the makings of a movie star or entertainer:

DISAPPOINTED WHEN ALL HOLLYWOOD HAD TO OFFER HER WAS A JOB AS [AN] EXTRA SHE GRAVITATED BACK TO NEW YORK TO BECOME A CABARET DANCER IN A CHEAP BROADWAY NIGHTCLUB, WHERE MACDONALD FIRST MADE HER ACQUAINTANCE.

As Godsell judged, Doris was "just another of those thrill-crazy girls who emerged from the dislocation of the last war." On her own she might not have

"A SCHEMING, MURDERING, ROBBING, COWARDLY, DOUBLE-CROSSING THUG, HIS ONLY THOUGHT WAS FOR HIMSELF AND HIS TENDER HIDE."

sunk to murder; seduced by George her downfall was inevitable. Although Mrs. MacDonald received a last-minute reprieve from the death sentence, she had to bear the news that her husband was to pay with his life. Godsell was satisfied that justice had been served: "Adelard Bouchard had been avenged, and the beautiful blonde who'd chosen the primrose path to perdition was left to pass the rest of her life behind the grilled bars of the prison cell with a number for a name."

Perhaps the biggest name in the annals of Canadian crime was Norman "Red" Ryan, a small-time thief who turned into a master bank robber. Chronicled in popular literature as "Canada's Master Criminal," the Toronto man had achieved fame primarily because of his celebrated bid to go

(facing page: Will Straw Collection)

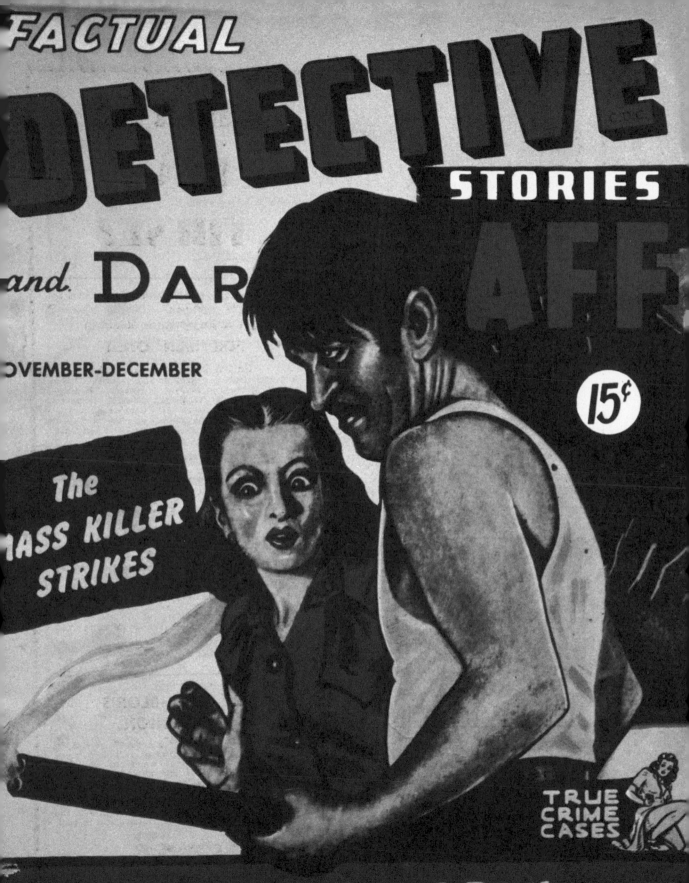

FACTUAL DETECTIVE STORIES

and DAR ... AFF

STORIES

NOVEMBER-DECEMBER

15¢

The MASS KILLER STRIKES

TRUE CRIME CASES

Boomerang Dollars of Death

straight, followed by a spectacular fall from grace in a botched bank robbery. Al Rucker, a true crime writer who had cut his authorial teeth as the editor of the 1930s tabloid *Week-ender*, brought a muckracking angle to his story of "Crookdom's Ace Phoney." Rucker's intent was to take the gloss off Ryan's colourful reputation: "Unfortunately, in spite of the now famous 'let down,' in which Ryan had duped everyone into thinking he had 'reformed,' Ryan's name is still synonymous with deeds of daring and criminal glamour." Rucker's tack was to counter that myth with evidence that Ryan had always been a coward and a police informer, ready to fink on fellow criminals in order to weasel favours from prison guards and policemen. As Rucker told it, Ryan was really "a 2-kt crook and a 16-jewel rat!"

Everyone, from Kingston's prison chaplain to the prime minister, took an interest in the progress of this charmer, convicted for a string of violent bank robberies in the second decade of the 20th century and through the 1920s. In 1923, after serving several terms in Kingston Penitentiary, Ryan was sentenced to life with 30 lashes. A mere 12 years later, influential backers persuaded the Remissions Branch to release the model prisoner. The supposedly repentant Ryan, posing happily with politicians and businessmen, had made a mockery of justice, Rucker commented: "No more ingenious diplomat has ever plotted the overthrow of Governments and Kings, than Red Ryan's plot to perpetrate the greatest hoax in criminal history." After his release he began to write his autobiography, called "Crime Doesn't Pay," and enjoyed life in the spotlight as Toronto's prodigal son. But the man proved unable to resist the thrill of ill-gotten gain. While keeping up the pretence of working as a hotel manager, he operated a car theft ring and carried out bank robberies. The last one, the botched holdup of a Sarnia liquor store, ended in a fatal encounter with the police. Rucker, in classic *True Police Cases* style, applauded the "phoney's" unglamorous end: "A scheming, murdering, robbing, cowardly, double-crossing thug, his only thought was for himself and his tender hide."

GAINING WISDOM

True crime readers who came of age in the Depression and the Second World War were well aware that getting by, let alone getting ahead, took tenacity and toil, but only if you played by the rules. The pulps supplied plenty of stories of men and women who broke the rules of civilized society, sometimes with panache, sometimes with brutality. If it took third-degree interrogations to flush out thieves from their "joints and dives," Canadian lawmen were up to the task. The craftiest crooks sometimes slipped away but criminals' greed — and their heedless generosity with other people's goods — eventually gave them away. Readers could thrill over cops-and-robbers cases and daydream in a railway waiting room or a barbershop about their own schemes to get rich quick. In the meantime, it was always possible to shell out a few dollars for a book that would explain how to become a popular dancer ("valuable as a business asset") or how to climb the "seven steps to personal success" — one at a time.

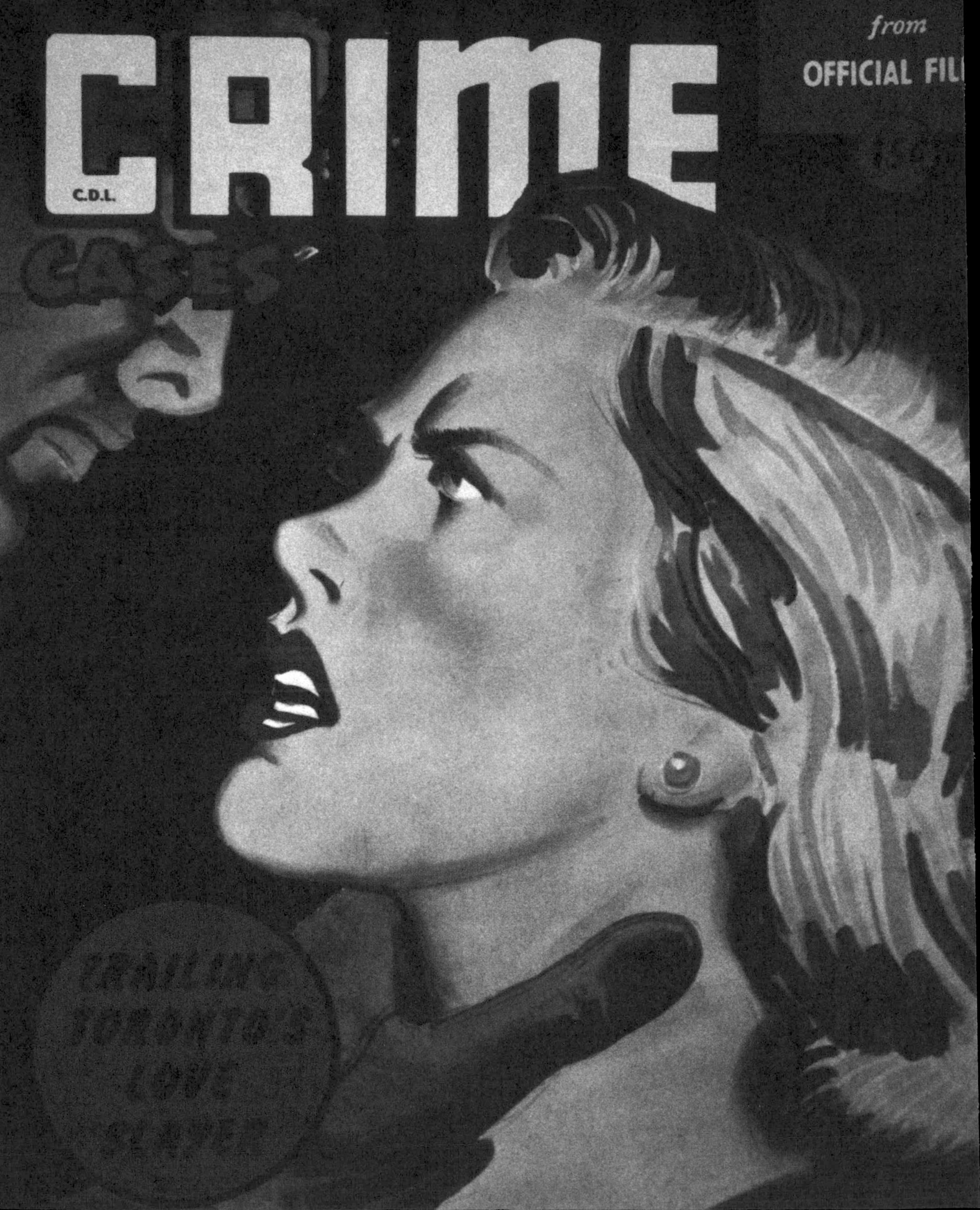

CRIME
C.D.L.
from
OFFICIAL

5

DEADLY SEX

TRUE CRIME MAGAZINE COVERS, with their nearly nude women and fearsome men, conveyed the impression that every story concerned deadly dealings between the sexes. Regular readers knew better. The average issue contained no more than a single case involving sexually tinged violence. While stories of love gone wrong, featuring jealous lovers, were commonplace, cases involving sex murders committed by dangerous strangers rarely inspired stories published — or publishable — in the Canadian pulps of the 1940s.

Rape and sexually motivated murder have always comprised a sub-theme of true crime literature, from 19th-century "penny dreadfuls" (the crimes of Jack the Ripper became instant bestsellers) to today's serial killer exposés. But they did not become a true crime magazine staple until the 1960s, when, along with cheap paperbacks and "sexploitation" films, they reoriented the genre toward its current fixation with sexual violence.

The 1940s was a transitional period: it was a time when brazenly sexual cover imagery promised more than it delivered. In fact, stories about "perverted" sexual violence were rare and sketchy. Those few stories published in the Canadian pulps (W. W. Bride seems to have been a specialist in the subgenre) adhered to the industry's unwritten code of propriety, steering clear of the frank and lurid accounts of sexual violence that dominate in today's true crime writing. Canadian writers wanting to explore "the sex perversion angle" had to seek out U.S. publishers, such as Ace and Dell.

While Canadian true crime covers did their best to make sexual danger look sexy, the few stories that touched on this theme were sober accounts, not sensational exposés. The typical deadly sex story involved a young innocent seized by a lust-crazed man. None of them dealt with cases in which the victim was a man or woman who had reached the age of majority. These stories added another angle to the "hunt" theme that ran through Canadian true crime pulps: they recounted how the police had trailed criminals who themselves were hunters — lone wolves on the lookout for easy prey.

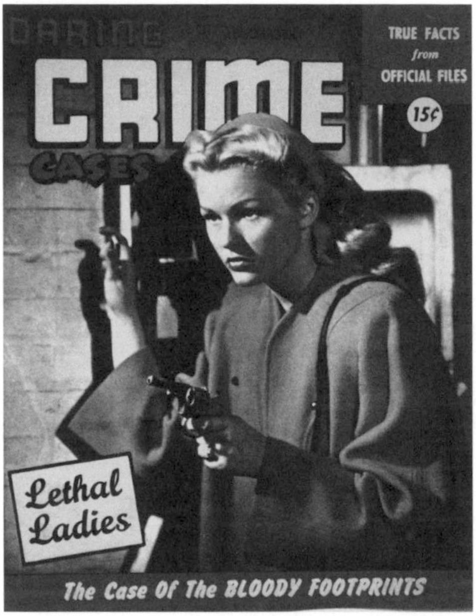
DARING
CRIME
CASES
TRUE FACTS
from
OFFICIAL FILES
15¢
Lethal
Ladies
The Case Of The BLOODY FOOTPRINTS

Although psychologists and psychiatrists had been working for decades to develop scientific explanations for sexual predation, true crime pulps of the 1940s relied on conventional moral explanations for "beastly" behaviour. Men who committed such offences were bad, not mad, even if experts and defence lawyers claimed to diagnose them as the latter. In the true crime genre, sex crime erupted when otherwise normal masculine heterosexual desire (the lustiness celebrated in bachelor's joke books) flared out of control. In the 1940s we see only the first hints of psychological explanations for deviance, an interpretive approach that would develop in 1950s paperbacks on "the abnormal."

All but one of the stories of "stranger danger" in the surviving Canadian pulps deals with a heterosexual rape-murder. Although medical and psychiatric experts of the 1940s had been exploring the psychological and hormonal etiology of homosexual psychopathy for a generation, pulp writers relied on old-fashioned terms like "fiend" and "degenerate" to describe sex killers. True crime stories briefly sketched defence counsels' attempts to mount insanity defences but the pulps stuck to the theory that men who preyed on innocents deserved punishment, not psychological therapy or medical treatment. Not until the very end of the decade, when homosexuality became a hot topic in paperbacks (Kinsey's path-breaking report on *Sexual Behaviour in the Human Male* was published in 1948, for instance) did detailed accounts of "deviant" sexual practices begin to circulate in popular literature.

Thus the typical 1940s true crime story of sexual murder barely distinguished between sexual violence and normal masculine behaviour: every element of a true crime pulp held that normal men dominated women because they were naturally overwhelmed by lust, inflamed by the objects of their desire. Alongside stories of sex crimes were ads that promised women could increase their "date appeal," while others declared that they could help men conquer "sexual slowness in women." Reproduced photos of victims, crime scenes and mug shots confirmed the horrible "truth" of sex murders, but grainy "specially posed" images added a bizarre romantic gloss to heterosexual violence. With their tantalizing cover images of alluring women, and misleadingly sentimental story titles such as "Trailing Toronto's Love Slayer," true crime magazines blurred the line between consensual romance and deadly desire.

VIRTUOUS VICTIMS

Nonlethal rape did not make its way into true crime magazines of the 1940s. As with robberies, only crimes leading to homicide turned cases into potential pulp fodder. But not just any sex murder would do. Every year in Canada, murders of prostitutes and "foreign" women (those outside the Anglo-Saxon mainstream) provided potential true crime material. Then as now, however, killings of unrespectable or marginalized women failed to inspire writers peddling murder stories. Cover images of women brimming with sex appeal sold magazines, but selling a story of sexual violence required a different kind of victim: a white young woman or a child of unblemished character.

Ruth Taylor, a 20-year-old Toronto clerk brutally killed on her way home from work, fitted the bill perfectly. She lived at home and contributed to the household economy during the darkest days of the Depression. One chilly November night in 1935 she left work at 11 p.m. but never made it home to her parents. W. W. Bride, the author of "Trailing Toronto's Love Slayer," carefully established that Taylor was not "the type to allow herself to be picked up by strangers." In fact, as the police discovered, "she was very reserved and quite dignified. A serious minded girl, her friends said. Her employers had nothing but praise for her." In other words, this young woman, unlike easy pickups, bore no responsibility for her fate.

Only one picture accompanied this story, published in *Daring Crime Cases* in 1946. While Bride described Taylor as "a pretty girl, even in death," the specially posed image took considerably more artistic licence. It showed a victim clad in a floral dress with a plunging neckline (Taylor had, in fact, worn a tweed coat and sweater to protect her from the early winter rain). Cradling the woman in his arms is a well-dressed man, leering hungrily at the woman's exposed neck and bosom. Readers of the mid-1940s would undoubtedly have recognized the model for this "specially posed" picture: the poster for the romantic blockbuster *Gone With the Wind*, released in 1939. This passionate image had no parallel in the text, however. Bride's dialogue was dry: "Was she assaulted?" the police inspector asks the coroner. "Cruelly and brutally," is the laconic reply.

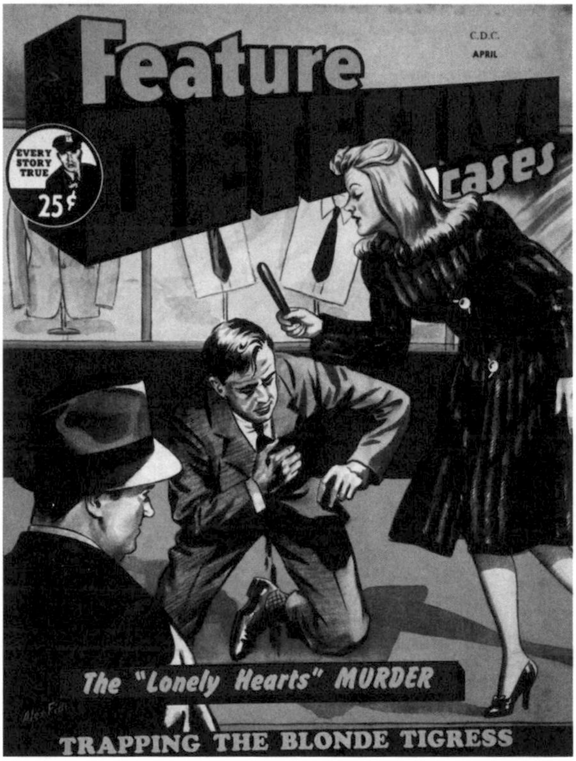
Feature
cases
C.D.C.
APRIL
EVERY STORY TRUE
25¢
The "Lonely Hearts" MURDER
TRAPPING THE BLONDE TIGRESS

Confirming attackers' cruelty turned on establishing victims' innocence. Youth and good looks certainly helped. Witness and police testimony about victims' habits and associates was critical, as well, but the victim in true crime stories of sexual violence was invariably attractive in an innocent rather than a knowing way. Whenever possible, stories about sex crimes included pictures taken from police files and newspaper offices. For instance, in Bride's story "The Bloody Knife Points to Death," 15-year-old victim Barbara Smith is pictured wearing a full-length, high-necked, long-sleeved dress — in 1945! Even the "school chums of innocent victim" Dorothy Hammond are pictured with "white veils haloing their heads" as they solemnly lead the 13-year-old's funeral procession in Edmonton. Both young women had been startled by strangers, who had knifed them to death. While their killers had overpowered them, the victims' reputations remained unsullied and thereby worthy of pity. Readers might well have shed a tear when they read that "dimpled, blonde, blue-eyed Dorothy Hammond, ice skater and choir singer," had died crying out, "Mama, Mama!"

The last words of nine-year-old John Benson remained a mystery, for he was found, like Ruth Taylor, bludgeoned and lifeless. Benson wasn't an urchin (the term Bride had used to describe the children who had found Taylor's body in a ravine). Rather, he was a good boy from a good family that had suffered already — his older brother had died fighting in France in the final months of the Second World War. Bride's account of the boy's discovery

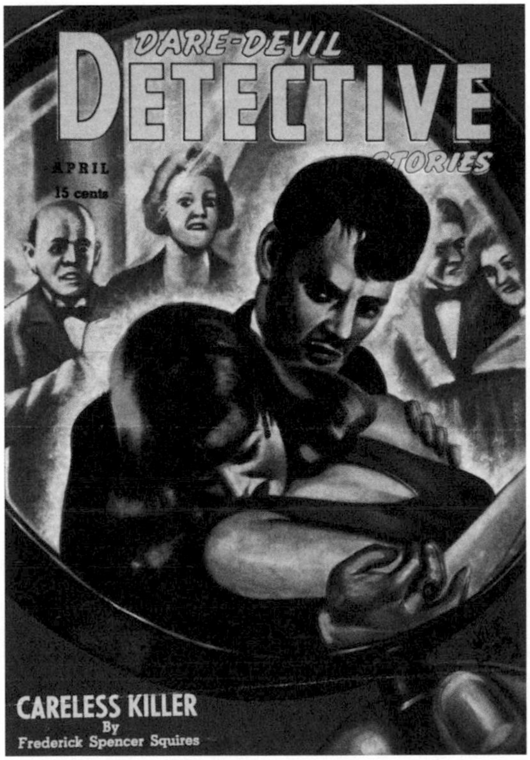
DARE-DEVIL
DETECTIVE
STORIES
APRIL
15 cents
CARELESS KILLER
By
Frederick Spencer Squires

CRADLING THE WOMAN IN HIS ARMS IS A WELL-DRESSED MAN, LEERING HUNGRILY AT THE WOMAN'S EXPOSED NECK AND BOSOM.

in the snow on Montreal's Mount Royal dramatized John's innocence: "Young hands they were, small and daintily formed, white and stiff in the cold." Unlike his "bullet-faced" attacker, introduced later in the story, Benson was a normal Canadian lad, who had met his death wearing a Montreal Canadiens jersey. A pulp *fiction* writer could not have invented more poignant material.

INNOCENTS ABROAD

All of the victims in "stranger danger" cases were killed because they were in the wrong place (a public setting, rather than their own homes) at the wrong time. True crime writers felt it necessary to explain that there was nothing fishy about victims' movements. By the mid-20th century, a generation after

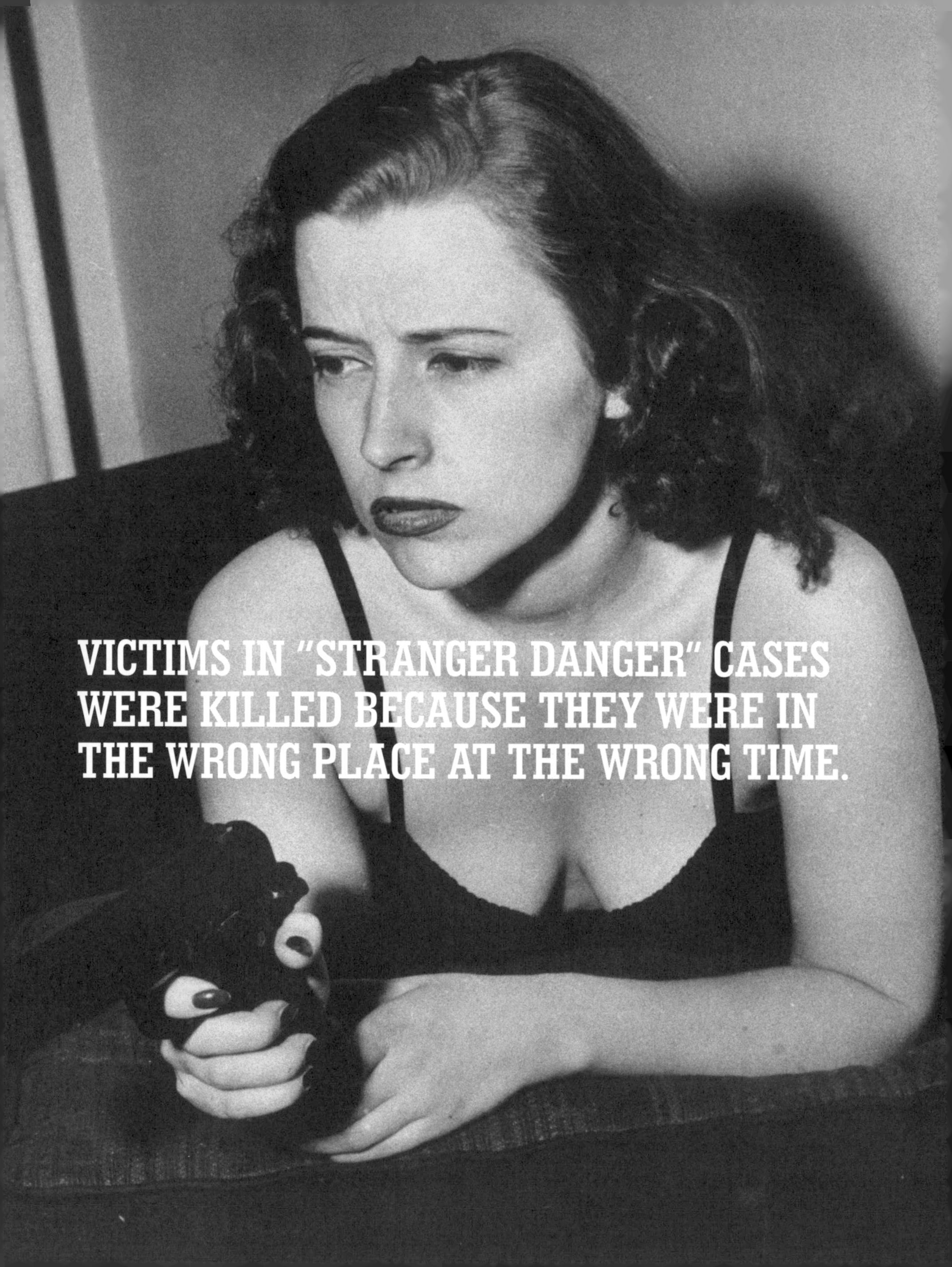
VICTIMS IN "STRANGER DANGER" CASES WERE KILLED BECAUSE THEY WERE IN THE WRONG PLACE AT THE WRONG TIME.

even respectable young people started "making whoopee," the mere presence of an unescorted woman on city streets at night did not automatically cast her in a suspicious light. And a young boy from a well-heeled family could hardly be faulted for spending a Saturday afternoon skiing. Nonetheless, writers felt compelled to emphasize that these victims, unlike their predatory killers, had not been out asking for trouble. The implications were chilling: Could anyone, even the virtuous, feel safe in a world of strangers?

FOR MEN ONLY?
THE GIRLS LOVE IT TOO !!
GALS
GAGS
PHOTOS
CARTOONS
4 BOOKS
EACH DIFFERENT!
MORE THAN 500 PAGES
only 1 BUCK!

Ruth Taylor had had an iron-clad excuse for being out late in downtown Toronto: her boss had asked her to work until 11 p.m. at the real estate firm where she clerked. When she left her office she had told her chum that "she was about all in and was going straight home." At that hour of the night she had had to take a short-turn streetcar that would drop her a mile from home. Bad timing and bad luck explained how victim and killer had met in the pouring rain. Borrowing from the tradition of classic melodrama, Bride described how a dutiful daughter had tragically died on her way back to her loving family — but this story was true. When Taylor's father identified her body he cried, "That's her. That's my little girl."

Young women out on the town were dubious candidates for depictions as bona fide victims, but by the 1940s it was possible for true crime writers to distinguish between doubtful pleasures and innocent pastimes. All of the "stranger danger" cases were set in Canada's cities, which offered citizens a wide range of commercial leisure pursuits. Thus, when Bride wrote about young women out on their own at night he dispensed with the judgemental tone of Victorian penny dreadfuls — at least when it came to respectable white females like Barbara Smith and Dorothy Hammond.

Both of these youngsters had been out to the pictures, an activity that had become a universal pastime by the war years. As Bride lamented in his story on Smith's murder, "a young girl's harmless walk ended in her horrible

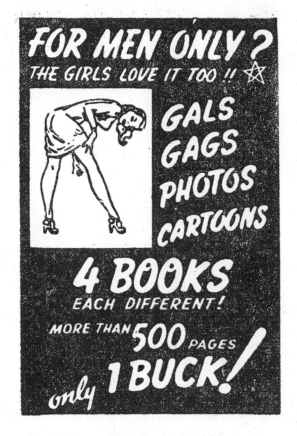

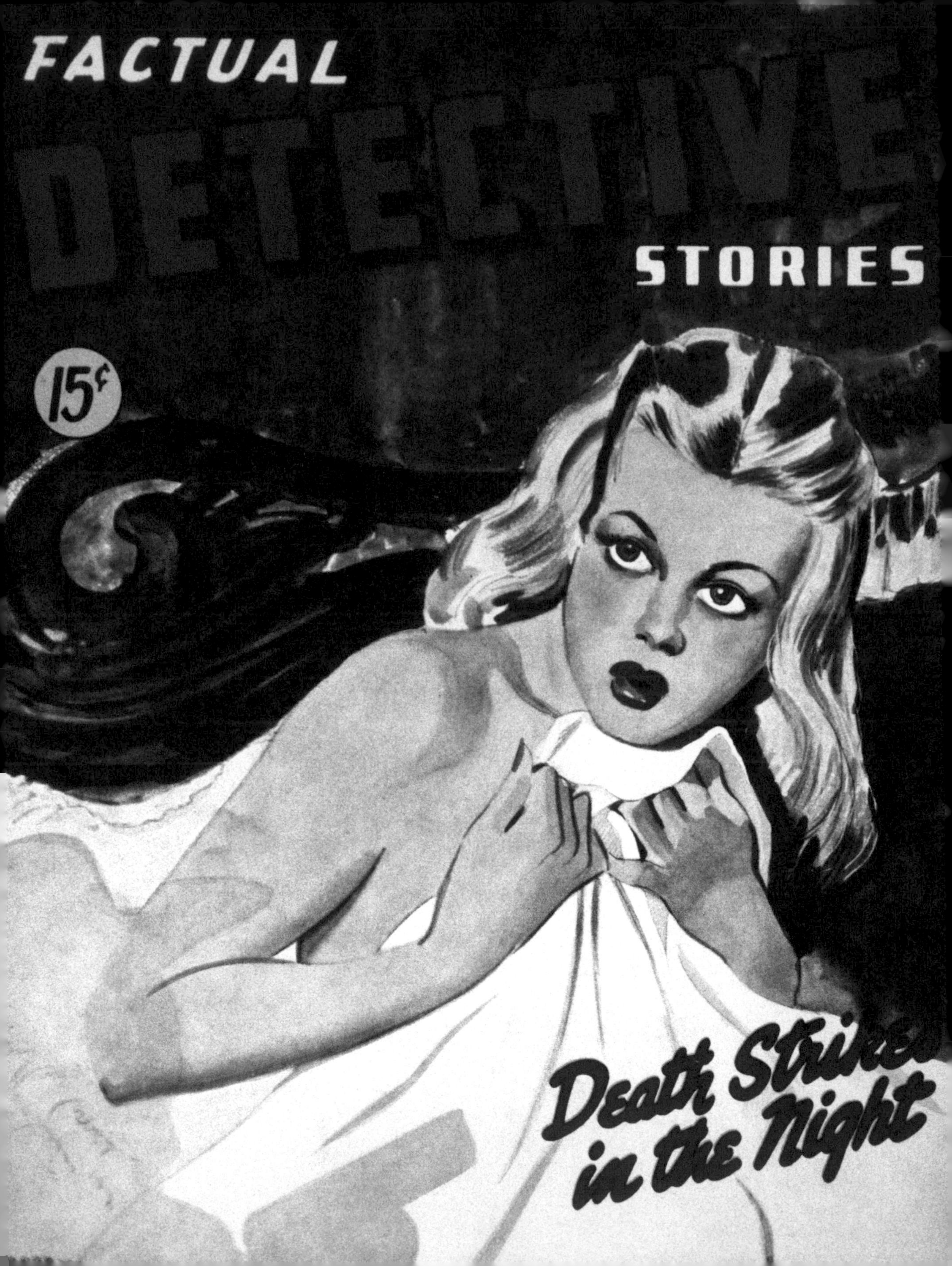
FACTUAL
DETECTIVE
STORIES
15¢
Death Strikes in the Night

murder." Besides, as her mother assured the police, "Barbara is a good girl. She doesn't go around with boys much." What movies had the two ventured out to see, without the slightest suspicion of their fates? Rita Hayworth in *Tonight and Every Night,* or perhaps *The Suspect,* starring Ella Raines and Charles Laughton?

Certainly Edmontonians, once they discovered the fate of Dorothy Hammond, treated the opening of her accused killer's trial like a sold-out show: "The crowd surges forward. Women scream as they are jammed in the doorway leading to the room where the trial is to be held … many who are unable to obtain seats are turned away." Here was a real-life chance to hear about a "young innocent's" fate and to see an instantly famous "fiend," Chester Johnson, charged with her murder. True crime magazine writers capitalized on Canadians' hunger for stories of ill-fated innocents, whether Hollywood fictions or local facts.

City living was a fact of life for most Canadians by the 1940s and stories of "stranger danger" confirmed urbanites' greatest fear: that in any "crowd of gay skiers," in any "brightly-lit café, on any lamp-lit slushy street," a murderer might blend into the crowd. Unlike "savage" Natives or ugly-faced "foreigners," these men depended on their ordinariness to pass unnoticed. If the police had trouble tracking them down *after* they killed, how could innocents abroad hope to look out for them?

> **SEX KILLERS WERE VILLAINS OF A SPECIAL ILK. THEY EVIDENTLY GAINED A TWISTED SENSE OF SATISFACTION FROM THEIR CRIMES, BUT THEY WERE NOT ANIMATED BY ORDINARY CRIMINAL IMPULSES SUCH AS JEALOUSY, GREED OR ENVY.**

89

LUST-MADDENED FIENDS

Sex killers were villains of a special ilk. They evidently gained a twisted sense of satisfaction from their crimes, but they were not animated by ordinary criminal impulses such as jealousy, greed or envy. Nor were they motivated by healthy male lust. Their curiously motivated crimes thus made them monstrous in the pages of the moralizing pulps. They were the bogeyman who haunted every child tutored on fairy tales. They were the shadowed stranger in film noir, the horrible voice broadcast in radio suspense dramas. They were everyone's worst nightmare come true.

What did the bogeyman look like? How did he behave? Troublingly, men like Harry O'Donnell and Chester Johnson had lived outwardly normal lives. O'Donnell was a married mechanic who had become a father shortly before he attacked Ruth Taylor. Johnson was a well-liked warehouse worker who lived with his grandparents. "His fellow workers and the neighbours who knew him well spoke nothing but good of him." Writer E. Davis described him favourably, as a "tall, good-looking chap with dark curly hair and a fine, well-built figure." His mug shots confirmed the description. W. W. Bride provided less detail about O'Donnell's looks, but he quoted a witness who said that the accused was always "immaculately dressed." Added to their respectable looks was the fact that neither man had betrayed any emotion during his trial. Johnson was "impassive and unmoved," while

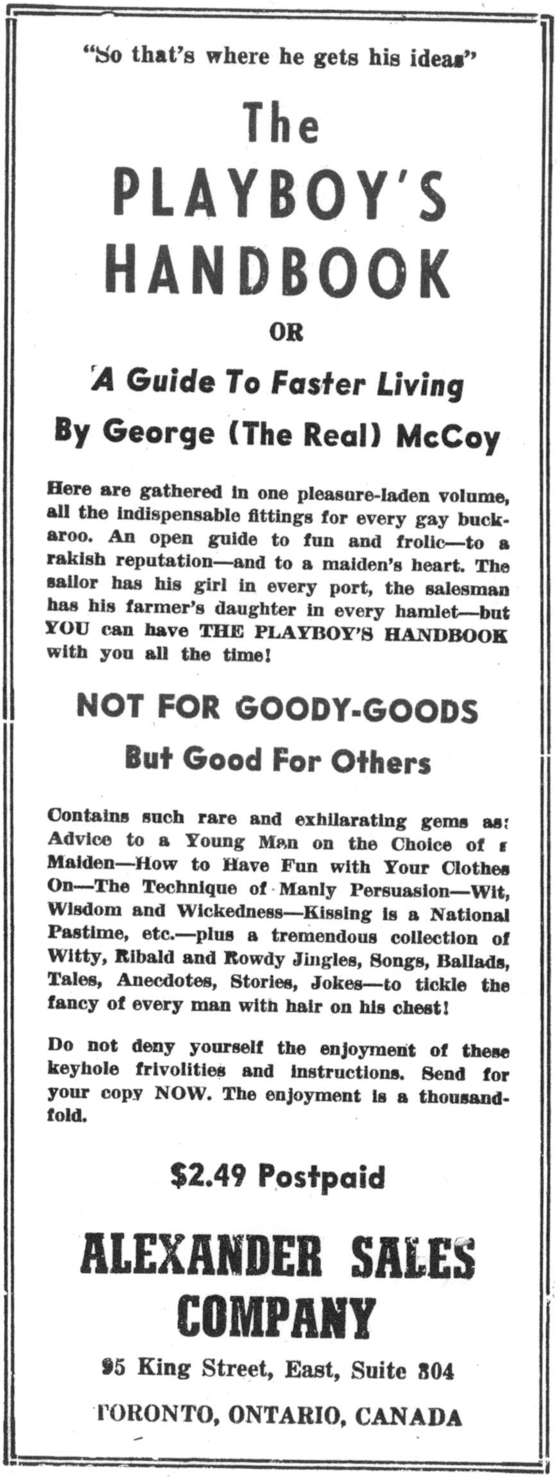
"So that's where he gets his ideas"
The PLAYBOY'S HANDBOOK
OR
A Guide To Faster Living
By George (The Real) McCoy
Here are gathered in one pleasure-laden volume, all the indispensable fittings for every gay buckaroo. An open guide to fun and frolic—to a rakish reputation—and to a maiden's heart. The sailor has his girl in every port, the salesman has his farmer's daughter in every hamlet—but YOU can have THE PLAYBOY'S HANDBOOK with you all the time!
NOT FOR GOODY-GOODS
But Good For Others
Contains such rare and exhilarating gems as: Advice to a Young Man on the Choice of a Maiden—How to Have Fun with Your Clothes On—The Technique of Manly Persuasion—Wit, Wisdom and Wickedness—Kissing is a National Pastime, etc.—plus a tremendous collection of Witty, Ribald and Rowdy Jingles, Songs, Ballads, Tales, Anecdotes, Stories, Jokes—to tickle the fancy of every man with hair on his chest!
Do not deny yourself the enjoyment of these keyhole frivolities and instructions. Send for your copy NOW. The enjoyment is a thousand-fold.
$2.49 Postpaid
ALEXANDER SALES COMPANY
95 King Street, East, Suite 304
TORONTO, ONTARIO, CANADA

O'Donnell appeared calm: "It was not natural." That men who looked so ordinary were capable of committing "fiendish" crimes made the successful police hunts in these cases all the more impressive, and consequently worthy of true crime reportage.

The killers of the Benson boy and Barbara Smith bore looks and demeanours that more closely fitted conventional cultural constructions of villainy. Roland Chasse, the man ultimately executed for Benson's murder, had earned the nickname "bullet face," on account of his acne. The cold stare in Chasse's mug shot was simply that of a white man, a bit rough around the edges, but hardly wild-eyed. Armand Proulx's picture did not appear in the story of Barbara Smith's death, but W. W. McBride (probably Bride) described him as a "tall, good-looking dark fellow." Here the code for evil designs was merely suggested by "darkness." In fact, Proulx was a Métis, a detail curiously absent in this account (especially in view of true crime's reliance on racial explanations for criminality). For both men, however, not even dark or rough looks betrayed the full extent of their evil inclinations, either at trial or at the time that they killed.

The evidence gathered by the police and presented at trial, not psychiatric testimony, was the key to unlocking the mystery behind these unprovoked attacks against women and children. While current-day true crime literature interrogates the mysteries of sociopathic and psychopathic behaviour, true crime writers of the 1940s showed little interest in probing sex killers' minds. Each one of the men whose crimes were recounted in the Canadian pulps was described in moral terms, as a "fiend" — "the lust-maddened fiend," the "fiend in human form," "the sex fiend," "the fiendish slayer." The term confirmed that only a congenitally evil person, an "enemy of mankind," could hunt down the purest and the weakest.

Explanations from the killer's own mouth offered all the insight that true crime magazines required. Chester Johnson had confessed that he had just felt "the urge to kill" when Dorothy Hammond had happened to cross his path. Chasse, true to his name, told the police that he had deliberately laid a trap for his victim, patiently waiting on the mountain for his quarry. He confessed that he had lured the Benson boy to a secluded area, kicked him and stabbed him, "and then I held my hand over his face until he went limp . . . When I was finished with him I buried his head in the snow." The ellipsis appeared in the published story, leaving a discreet blank in the tale. Only a keen-eyed reader would have discerned that the murderer had sexually assaulted the boy. Although the story of "The Body on the Mountain"

"THE MIRACLE BOOK – FOR A NEW AND BRIGHTER TOMORROW" What did men do before Viagra? They ordered books advertised in pulps, such as Secrets of the Male Hormone, which promised to reveal "the startling possibilities of restoring manhood." The manual pledged to "restore sanity to men who suffer male hormone hunger." As the headline hinted, however, "it's too good to be true."

91

includes a great deal of information about the physical evidence and the undercover operations that led to Chasse's arrest, the only description of the assault itself is contained in a few suggestive words: the boy had been the "victim of a pervert," and he had been stabbed in the "groin."

Writers' references to heterosexual assault were equally coded. Mentioning undergarments seems to have sufficed to indicate rape. Barbara Smith had to identify her sister through "a pair of panties" found at the death scene, while the condition of Ruth Taylor's clothing spoke volumes: "Her underwear lay damp, torn and soggy against the cold flesh. Over to one side, lay a torn black skirt." Both demure and teasing, the true crime pulps of the 1940s condemned deadly sex only in its most monstrous form: the chance encounter that brought innocence into the company of evil. As a *Stag Magazine* advertisement ("for the sophisticated stag") that appeared alongside the story of Chester Johnson's crime suggested, masculine lust was "A OK." Here the mingling of moralizing text and titillating ads captured the incongruous character of the true crime pulps.

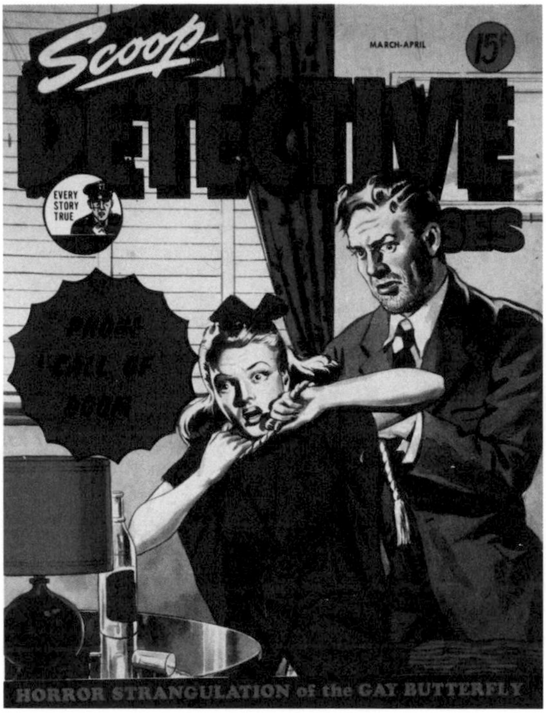
Scoop
DETECTIVE
MARCH-APRIL
15¢
EVERY STORY TRUE
HORROR STRANGULATION of the GAY BUTTERFLY

CROSSING THE LINE

If Canadian pulps carefully steered around the full extent of violence committed upon victims, preferring to fill stories with old-fashioned condemnations of evil, U.S. true crime magazines provided an outlet for more modern accounts of sexual violence. This was evident in Philip Godsell's "The Murdering Monster and the Playground of Doom," published in one of the Dell publications, *Inside Detective*, in 1947. In this exploration of homosexual murder Godsell covered not one but two lethal assaults, which had led to the deaths of young "curly-haired" boys in Vancouver and Calgary in 1946. More significantly, the story dealt frankly with the nature of the attacks and even explored the psychosocial origins of the killer's motivation.

Published in the same period as "Trailing Toronto's Love Slayer" and the other stories discussed above, "The Murdering Monster" relied on the same conventions as the material published in the Canadian pulps including the Gothic language of "monstrosity." In one case, a boy in Vancouver had been out for a swim in Stanley Park's Lost Lagoon; in the other, a lad had been seized while visiting a Calgary amusement park. In these public places,

PULP WRITERS RELIED ON OLD-FASHIONED TERMS LIKE "FIEND" AND "DEGENERATE" TO DESCRIBE SEX KILLERS.

FACTUAL
DETECTIVE
STORIES
BLAIRMORE'S
MURDERING
BOOTLEGGER
AUGUST
15 Cents
"EMPEROR PIC," uncrowned king of the Crow's Nest.
FLORENCE LASSANDA. Was she the girl in the scarlet tam?
THE BODY IN THE SAND PIT
TRUE CRIME STORIES
SEX FIENDS TERRORIZE CHICAGO

where strangers circulated, witnesses reported that they had seen a tall, thin man talking with the boys shortly before they had disappeared. As usual, superior policing, as well as cooperation between the Vancouver and Calgary police, had allowed detectives to trace the movements of a recently discharged soldier who was serving time in Lethbridge for a burglary. Inquiries into the man's military record disclosed that he had been court-martialled

COVER IMAGES OF WOMEN BRIMMING WITH SEXUAL APPEAL SOLD MAGAZINES, BUT SELLING A STORY OF SEXUAL VIOLENCE REQUIRED A DIFFERENT KIND OF VICTIM: A WHITE YOUNG WOMAN OF UNBLEMISHED CHARACTER.

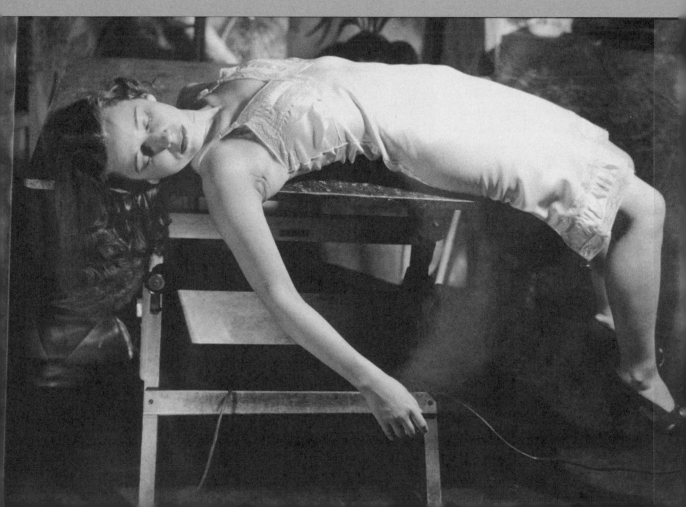

overseas "for offences against boys." Once Calgary's Inspector Boyd confronted the suspect, "the sordid story of a sex pervert's irrepressible urge to kill" unfolded.

One of the key distinctions between this story and the ones published in Canadian true crime magazines was Godsell's extensive use of Donald Staley's detailed and psychologically oriented confession. In a "slow monotonous voice" the tortured man had unloaded his burden to the Calgary police. Describing his attack on young Garry Billings, Staley said: "I grabbed him from behind the throat and tried to strangle him. He wouldn't stop kicking so I stabbed him repeatedly with my knife . . . I'd lost my self control. I then committed sodomy on him." Explicit passages such as these, written in the first person, placed the reader inside the killer's head, providing the murderer's perspective on the criminal act rather than the lawman's subsequent construction of the case. In other words, this was not true crime Canadian-style.

Most noteworthy, however, was the space Godsell devoted to Staley's explanation for his uncontrollable impulses. Drawing from both the confession and his lawyer's (ultimately unsuccessful) arguments that his client was insane, Godsell traced Staley's criminal impulses to his history of sexual abuse in orphanages and later in juvenile and adult detention facilities: "It was there that I learned sexual perversion from other boys when I was around seven," the suspect had explained. Staley's lawyer, John S. Mavor, presented his client as a victim of the social cancer of institutional neglect: "'society as a whole is on trial.'"

Statements of this sort were uttered in many North American courtrooms by the 1940s, but Canadian true crime magazine stories of the decade were not prepared to explore psychological or social explanations for deadly sexual dealings. That time would arrive, but well after the heyday of the pulps.

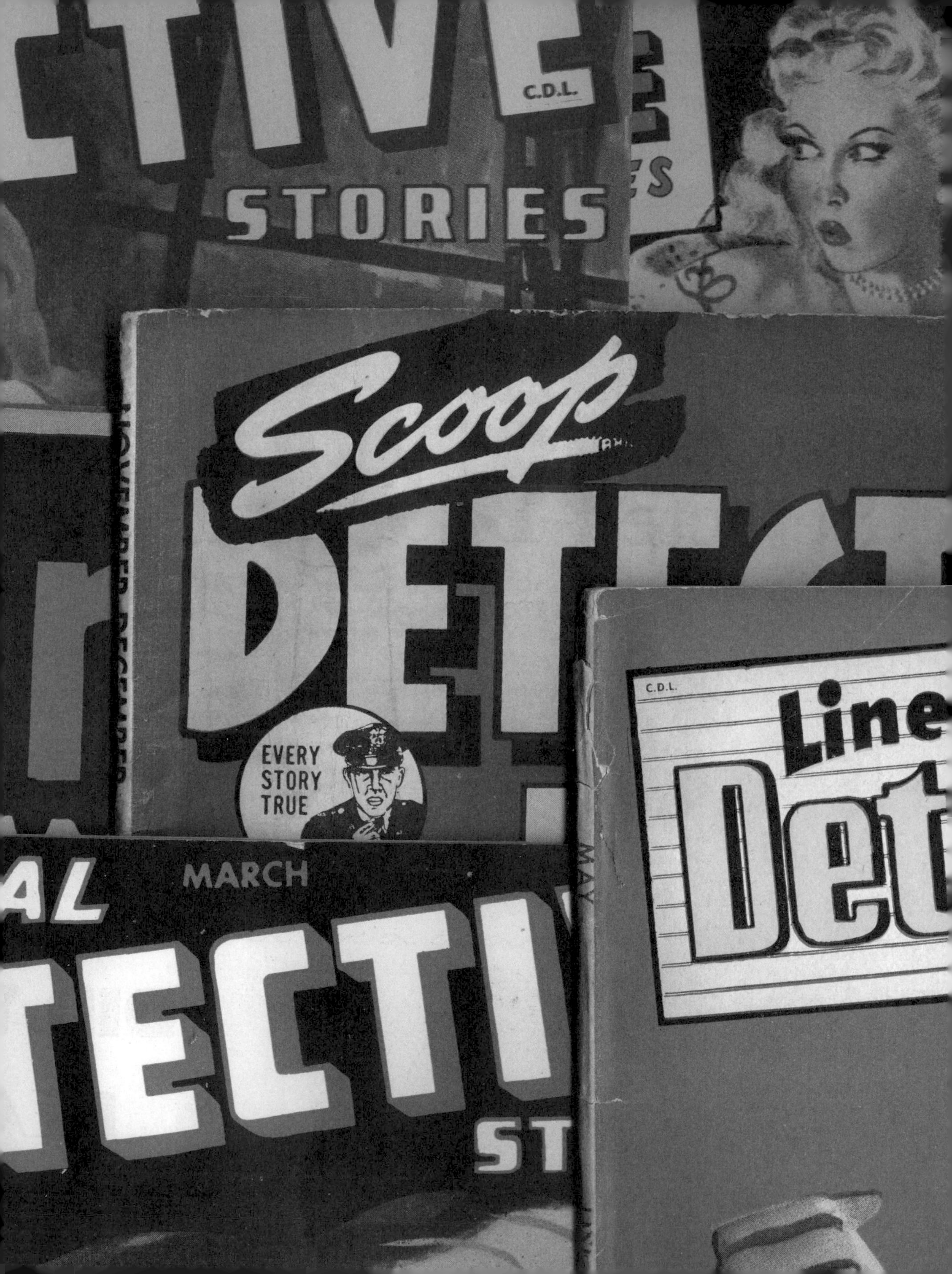

CTIVE
C.D.L.
STORIES
Scoop
EVERY STORY TRUE
MARCH
AL
TECTI
ST
C.D.L.
Line
Det
MAY

6

FADE TO GREY: THE END OF AN INDUSTRY AND AN ERA

IN SOME RESPECTS the war's end ushered in a period of optimism: the forces of evil had been confronted and defeated, and Canada was happily on the winning side. Yet uncertainty clouded that rosy outlook. The good guys had dropped bombs that had introduced the world to the nuclear era. And had all that consorting with Stalin during the war set fifth columnists into the midst of North American life?

During the 1940s, pulp magazines had provided a cheap and thrilling diversion from the horrors of war, most of which became fully known only after the battles were over. While crimes far greater in magnitude than local bank robberies or domestic shootouts were revealed, Canadians didn't lose their taste for true crime stories. They certainly had more to choose from, as wartime importation bans were lifted and U.S. magazines flooded the newsstands once again. For a few years Canadians could still read about murders committed in places like Fort Resolution in the few local pulps that survived, including *Factual Detective Stories* and *Famous Crime Cases*, but the heyday of the Canadian pulps came to a close by the early 1950s.

Over the 1940s, Canadian publishers had imitated an American art form, splashing sex and violence on risqué covers and inserting advertisements for books that respectable people wouldn't have dreamed of buying in a shop. But the repackaging of real crimes as true crime stories was far more restrained. In the black-and-white world of Canadian true crime, readers encountered the message that law and order would always prevail, and that

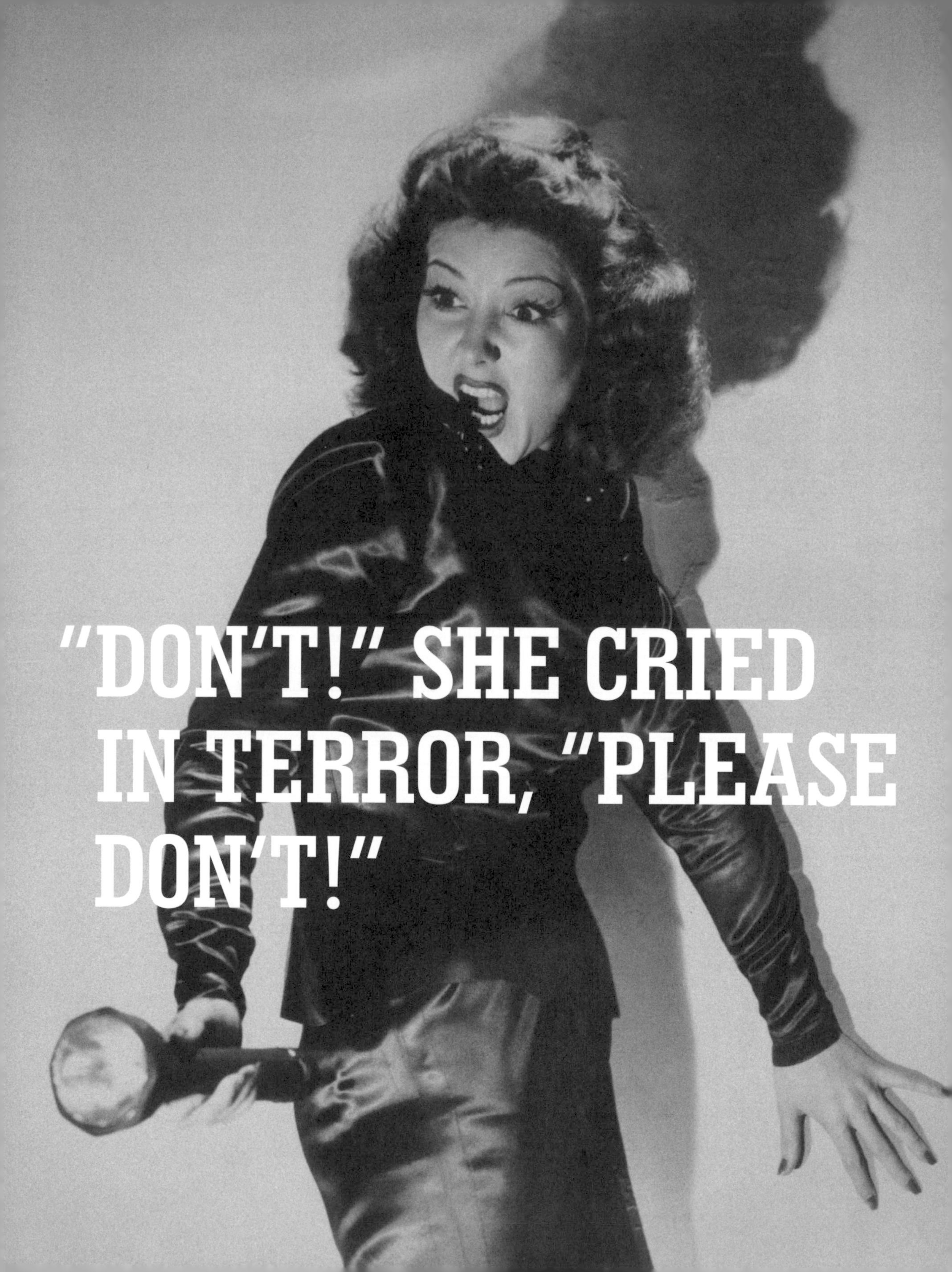
"DON'T!" SHE CRIED
IN TERROR, "PLEASE
DON'T!"

justice would ultimately triumph, thanks to the dedication of brainy lawmen, the foremost of whom were those archetypal Canadian good guys, the Mounties. Moreover, readers could also take comfort in the fact that if evil existed, it emanated from predictable sources: the prideful Indian, the fickle woman, the passionate French Canadian, the greedy American, the over-sexed brute. Only by the decade's end, as stories about "psychopaths" began to find their way into Canadian magazines, did writers explore the more chilling thought — that evil lurked among the apparently normal, the everyday.

If Canadians wanted to learn more about local crimes in the postwar era they would not have true crime pulps to consult. By the 1950s it was back to newspapers, or to book collections of famous crimes and criminals (for those who could afford them). But the decline of Canadian pulps was part of a broader phenomenon that led to the death of the U.S. pulps, as well. A product of changing tastes and markets, the pulp magazine became obsolete by the late 1950s. Against these postwar cultural and economic forces the local true crime magazine industry was no match.

True crime magazines watered the seeds of their own destruction when they advertised cheap paperbacks. By the 1950s, drugstore magazine racks were replaced by revolving kiosks full of sizzling novels such as *Reform School Girl* or *Diana*, the "autobiography of a strange wayward woman." True crime magazines were overshadowed by hard-boiled police and detective novels, as well as by film and television shows, such as *Dragnet*. Canadian content did not disappear but emerged in other formats, including nationally distributed scandal sheets, such as *Flash*, *Hush*, *Justice* and *Police Patrol*. The market for high-minded police procedurals had shrunk in the face of these more cynical and sexually frank explorations of crime. With their stilted style and rigid moralism, magazines like *Factual Detective*, popular in the 1940s, seemed old-fashioned only a decade later.

The true crime industry continues to flourish today, albeit in different forms. Collections of "famous Canadian cases" are still published regularly but Canadians are more likely to consume their true crime in CBC-produced movies such as *The Boys of St. Vincent*, *Butterbox Babies*, *The Helen Betty Osborne Story*, *The David Milgaard Story* and *Love and Hate*. The last of these, the story of Saskatchewan politician and rancher Colin Thatcher's conviction for the murder of his estranged wife, Jo Ann Wilson, continues to explore the enduring theme of "love gone wrong." But the other films confront issues that 1940s Canadian pulps steered clear of — state crime, racism, police incompetence and wrongful convictions. In the post-pulp era

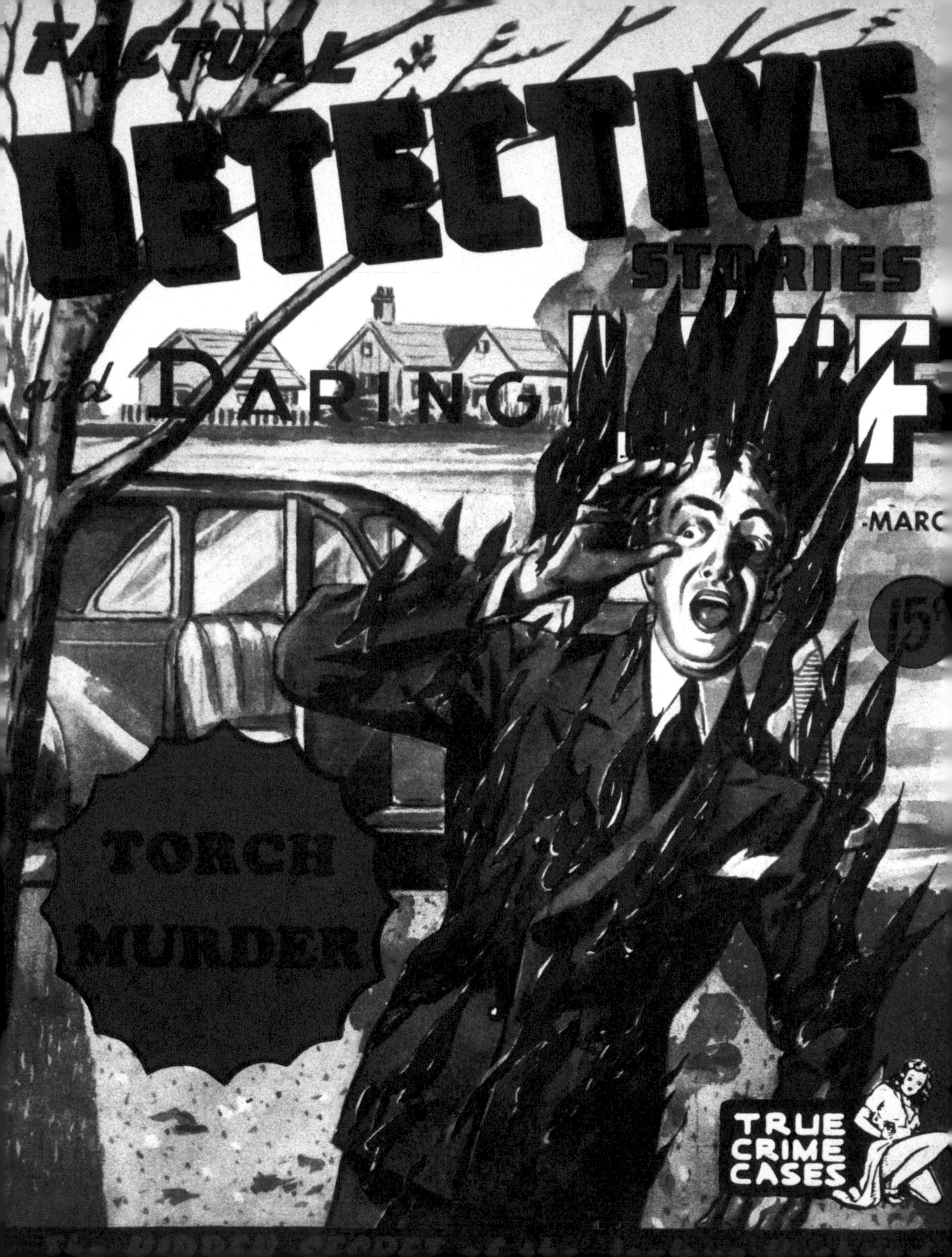

FACTUAL
DETECTIVE
STORIES
and DARING
MARC
15¢
TORCH MURDER
TRUE CRIME CASES

the scope for antiheroes has broadened while the image of infallible justice has faltered, with Royal Commissions into RCMP wrongdoing and media exposure of law enforcement's "deals with devils" such as killer Karla Homolka in Ontario. If any figure claims heroic status these days it's the crusading coroner, such as television's Dominic DaVinci, not the detective. Yet even miraculous advances in forensic science can't make up for incompetence and corruption

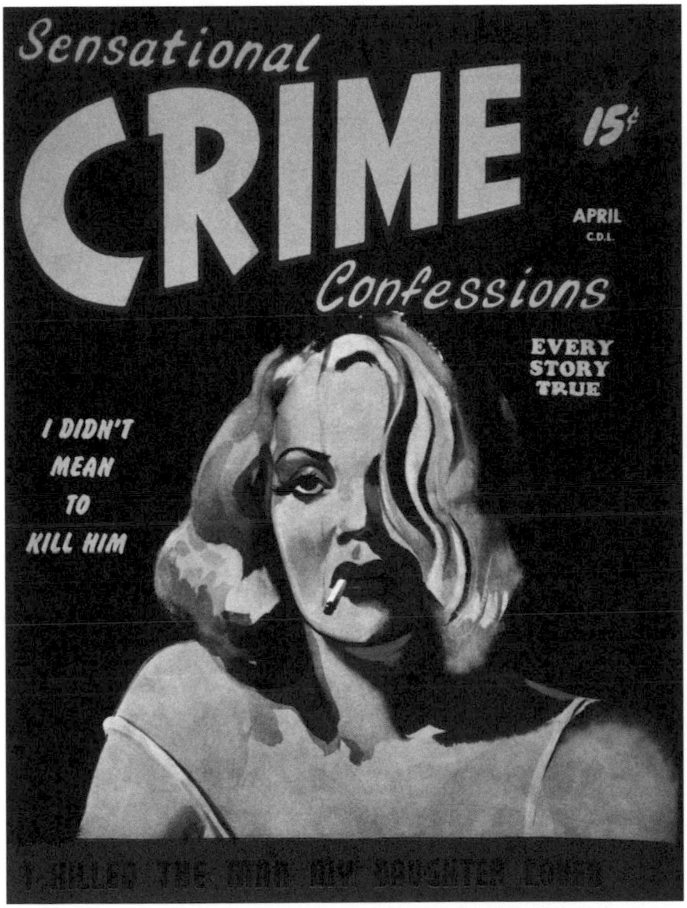
Sensational
CRIME
15¢
APRIL
C.D.L.
Confessions
EVERY STORY TRUE
I DIDN'T MEAN TO KILL HIM

TRUE CRIME MAGAZINES WERE OVERSHADOWED BY HARD-BOILED POLICE AND DETECTIVE NOVELS, AS WELL AS BY FILM AND TELEVISION SHOWS, SUCH AS DRAGNET.

(exhaustively detailed in *Redrum the Innocent*, the story of the Christine Jessup murder investigation in Ontario and Guy Paul Morin's wrongful conviction).

While revisiting old cases of possible or probable wrongful convictions is one stream of current-day true crime, another springs from a desire to induce sympathy for redeemable sorts who suffered harsh justice. For example, British Columbia poet Susan Musgrave wrote on behalf of her husband,

Stephen Reid, whose criminal backsliding drew intense media coverage. The robber-turned-novelist, the one-time leader of the colourful "Stopwatch Gang" in the 1970s and '80s, a group credited with stealing more than $15 million, had slipped back into armed robbery. Reconvicted in 1999 and sentenced to 18 years in prison, Reid has also published accounts of his fall from respectability, attributing it to his struggle with drug addiction. In some cases, recent portrayals of true crime have recast convicted killers as victims whose lives are stories of oppression. For example, John Estacio and John Murrell's opera *Filumena*, the latest rendition of Florence Lassandro's case, likens the executed woman's fate to the immigrant's thwarted search for freedom and acceptance on the vast Canadian Prairies. In this controversial but critically acclaimed production mounted in 2003, Filumena flees a loveless marriage, only to become involved with Emperor Pic and his bootlegging gang. Together they struggle against social exclusion and pursue their dream of a better life for themselves and their fellow Italians. As the *Globe and Mail*'s arts critic observed, "by the end the principals are so ennobled that you almost forget they're killers." The geography hasn't changed, but the moral compass has gone haywire.

So it goes with greed, as well. The rise of consumerism as the main engine of the domestic economy in the post-war era provided a starkly different context for true crime storytelling. Gone was the Depression's austerity and the sacrifices of the war. As the standard of living rose in North America in the 1950s and '60s, comfort and ease were acquired largely on credit. As advertisements for ocean cruises and luxury vehicles croon, the high life can be consumed today and paid for some time in the future. In 1940s true crime pulps, men and women who had aspired to wealth without work were headed for jail or the gallows, not meetings with creditors. Recent accounts of murdering robbers tend to play up their daring criminal exploits, or in some cases underline former crooks' capacity to reform — morally ambiguous story elements that Canadian true crime pulp editors would have flatly rejected a half century earlier.

By contemporary standards the 1940s was still a remarkably innocent era when it came to sexuality. Pulps of that era incorporated intentionally sexy art to package comparatively prudish stories. Not until the end of the '40s did overt discussion of sexual matters begin to creep in. Even book advertisements had tiptoed around subject matter available for "adults only." For instance, the book summary for *Diana* (advertised throughout the 1940s in Canadian true crime pulps) did not use the "L" word until late in the decade, by which time it promised to answer the vexing question, "Who, or WHAT, is a Lesbian?" Even rare stories of sexual assaults were written in veiled terms that relied on the reader's imagination. By the 1950s, when Kinsey's reports on male and female sexuality circulated in cheap editions and when sizzling paperbacks on sexual "deviants" could be purchased for little more than a magazine had cost, the true crime pulps of the previous decade seemed stiff and coy.

Now it is no longer necessary to purchase mail order issues of books delivered in plain brown wrapping paper in order to read every last detail of a sexual attack. Indeed, according to feminist critics we have entered "the age of sex crime," in which accounts of sexually depraved murderers dominate both true crime and fiction in print and film, and on the internet. In a curious combination of childish pastimes and the commercial exploitation of horrible crimes, it is currently possible to purchase serial-killer trading cards and to trade with other collectors online.

Perhaps this is why the pulps of the 1940s strike a nostalgic as well as kitschy chord. Not only is the artwork garishly alluring but the stories present a world free of doubt, ambiguity and uncertainty. The moral lines sketched in the stories were every bit as stark as the bold strokes on the magazine covers. Real crimes, certainly, but not the real world.

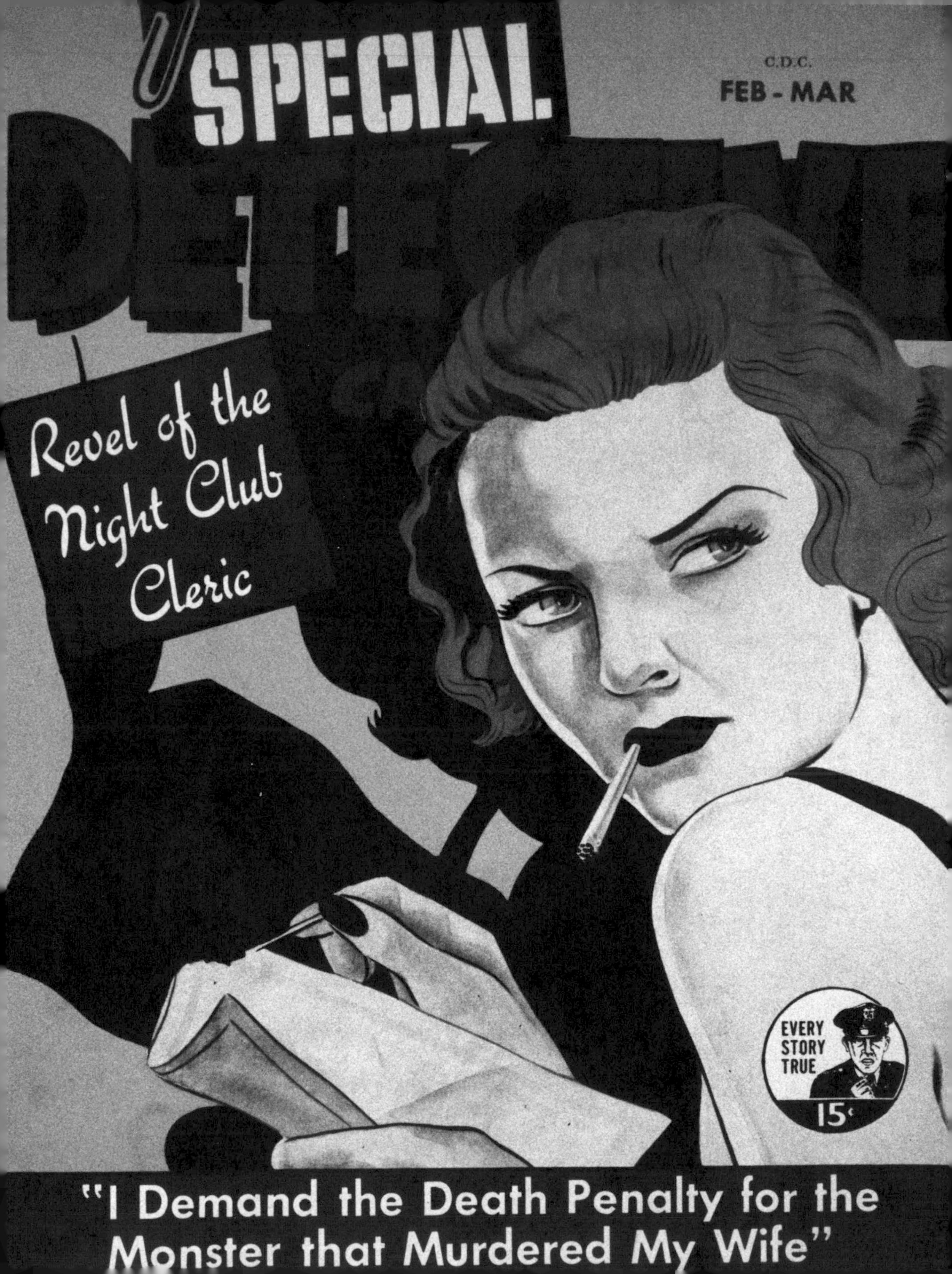
SPECIAL
C.D.C.
FEB - MAR
Revel of the Night Club Cleric
EVERY STORY TRUE
15¢
"I Demand the Death Penalty for the Monster that Murdered My Wife"

ACKNOWLEDGEMENTS

THE STORY YOU'VE JUST READ is true: only the names have been removed to protect the innocent. *True Crime, True North* would not have been possible without the help and good humour of a number of people whose covers we're now happy to blow. Annalee Greenberg, editor of *The Beaver*, revealed the existence of a large stash of Canadian pulps in the National Library of Canada and encouraged us to write this book. Michel Brisebois, the National Library's rare books librarian, made the research even more enjoyable than it already was, allowing us to rifle through his collection and disrupt his otherwise quiet reading room with our gales of laughter and snorts of disbelief as we came across yet another ad for steak knives, date blouses or the cuisine de l'amour. Jim Bowman of the Glenbow Archives facilitated our access to the Philip H. Godsell Fonds and generously accommodated our requests for endless photocopies and photographs. The archivists at the National Archives of Canada helped us navigate the complexities of the access restrictions for Department of Justice material and sped our research as a result.

Chris Petrusic did some fine research for us in Ottawa, tracking down true crime stories and ads with a level of determination worthy of any steely-eyed Mountie. Susan Houston, Will Straw of McGill University, George Flie and Nelson Ball were kind enough to share their knowledge and swag with us, and the book is better as a result. Carole Gerson and the History of the Book in Canada Project, as well as a Social Sciences and Humanities Research Council of Canada Small Grant from Simon Fraser University, provided support both intellectual and financial.

Jean Wilson and Mary Lynn Young provided us with some much-needed "publishing for dummies" advice when it was time for two academics to test the waters of the trade world. The Raincoast gang has been a joy to work with: thanks to Lynn Henry, Michelle Benjamin, Jesse Finkelstein and our editor Derek Fairbridge, for their boundless enthusiasm and support. Eileen Mak provided some last minute proofreading. Bill Douglas of "The Bang" couldn't have worked for any pulp magazine as the in-house artist and designer — he's too good. We're fortunate to have him.

Finally, like the men in scarlet, we know that any success comes from the result of teamwork. So we thank each other — and, of course, Mickey.

Carolyn Strange and *Tina Loo*

BIBLIOGRAPHY

STATUTES

Canada. *Statutes of Canada*. 1940, 4-5 Geo. 5, c. Chap. 2, An Act Respecting the Conservation of Exchange.

ARCHIVAL SOURCES

National Archives of Canada. RG 13, vol. 1601 (O'Donnell), vol. 1944 (Cashel).

National Library of Canada. Pulp Art and Fiction Collection.

IMAGE CREDITS

Unless otherwise noted, all images contained in this book are from the National Library of Canada, Pulp Art Collection. All black and white photographs are B-movie stills found in the "Cheesecake Photos" file (see p. 25) contained in that collection.

INTERVIEWS

Flie, George. Interview by Carolyn Strange. Toronto, August 2001.

Ball, Nelson. Interview by Carolyn Strange. Toronto, August 2003.

INTERNET SOURCES

The Culture of Cities: Print Culture and Urban Visuality website.
http://www.arts.mcgill.ca/ahcs/cultureofcities/Print%20Culture.html

SECONDARY SOURCES

Adams, Mary Louise (1995)
"Youth, Corruptibility, and English-Canadian Postwar Campaigns against Indecency," *Journal of the History of Sexuality*, vol. 6, 1: 89-117

Barker, Martin (1989)
Comic: Ideology, Power and the Critics. Manchester, Manchester University Press

Bell, Charles W. (1935)
Who Said Murder? Toronto, Macmillan

Bell, John, ed. (1996)
Canuck Comics (foreword Harlan Ellison). Downsview, Ontario, Matrix Books

Berton, Pierre (1975)
Hollywood's Canada: The Americanization of Our National Image. Toronto, McClelland and Stewart

Biressi, Anita (2001)
Crime, Fear and the Law in True Crime Stories. Basingstoke, Palgrave

Bloom, Clive (1996)
Cult Fiction: Popular Reading and Pulp Theory. London, Macmillan

Cameron, Deborah (1990)
"Pleasure and Danger, Sex and Death," in Day, George, ed., *Readings in Popular Culture.* London, Macmillan

Cameron, Deborah and Elizabeth Fraser (1987)
The Lust to Kill: a Feminist Investigation of Sexual Murder. New York, New York University Press

Caputi, Jane (1987)
The Age of Sex Crime. Bowling Green, Ohio, Bowling Green University Press

Dawson, Michael (1997)
"'That nice red coat goes to my head like champagne': Gender, Antimodernism and the Mountie Image, 1880-1960," *Journal of Canadian Studies*, vol. 32, 3: 119-39

_____ (1998)
The Mountie from Dime Novel to Disney. Toronto, Between the Lines

Day, George, ed. (1990)
Readings in Popular Culture: Trivial Pursuits? London, Macmillan

Einstadter, Werner and Stuart Henry (1995)
Criminological Theory: An Analysis of Its Underlying Assumptions. Fort Worth, Texas, Harcourt Brace College Publishers

Guillet, Edwin C. (1943)
This Man Hanged Himself: A Study of the Evidence in the King versus Newell. Toronto, Ontario, Ontario Publishing Co.

Halttunen, Karen (1998)
Murder Most Foul: The Killer and the American Gothic Imagination. Cambridge, Harvard University Press

Haste, Steve (1997)
Criminal Sentences: True Crime in Fiction and Drama. London, Signus Arts

Hays, Michael, and Anastasia Nikolopoulou, eds. (1996) *Melodrama: the Emergence of a Genre.* New York, St. Martin's

Hines, Max (1998)
Canadian Crimes. Toronto, Viking

Hutchinson, Don, ed. (1998)
Scarlet Riders: Pulp Fiction Tales of the Mounties. Oakville, Ontario, Mosaic Press

Hutchings, Peter (2001)
The Criminal Spectre in Law, Literature and Aesthetics, 2001, London: Routledge

Ingebretsen, Edward J. (1998)
"The Monster in the Home: True Crime and the Traffic in Body Parts," *Journal of American Culture*, vol. 21, 1 (Spring): 27-34

Lesser, Robert (1997)
Pulp Art: Original Cover Paintings for the Great American Pulp Magazines. New York, Grammercy Books

Mandel, Ernest (1984)
Delightful Murder: A Social History of the Crime Story. London, Pluto

Macleod, R. C. (1976)
The North West Mounted Police and Law Enforcement, 1873-1905. Toronto, University of Toronto Press

Macpherson, M. A. (1999)
Outlaws of the Canadian West. Edmonton, Lone Pine

McCormack, William, with Bob Cooper (1998)
Life on Homicide: A Police Detective's Memoire. Toronto, Stoddart

Muller, Eddie (1998)
Dark City: The Lost World of Film Noire. New York, St. Martin's

n.a (1983)
Outlaws and Lawmen of Western Canada, vol. 2. Surrey, British Columbia, Frontier Books

Newman, Graeme (1990)
"Popular Culture and Criminal Justice: A Preliminary Inquiry," *Journal of Criminal Justice,* vol. 18, 3 261-74

Patterson, T. W. (1977)
Outlaws of Western Canada: A Collection of Canada's Most Villainous Outlaws. Langley, British Columbia, Stagecoach

Robin, Martin (1982)
The Saga of Red Ryan, and Other Tales of Violence from Canada's Past. Saskatoon, Western Producer Prairie Books

Server, Lee (1993)
Danger is My Business: An Illustrated History of the Fabulous Pulp Magazines, 1896-1953. San Francisco, Chronicle Books

Skene-Melvin, David, ed. (1994)
Crime in a Cold Climate: An Anthology of

Classic Canadian Crime. Toronto, Simon and Pierre

Smith, Barbara (1994)
Fatal Intentions: True Canadian Crime Stories. Toronto, Hounslow

Soothill, Keith, and Sylvia Walby (1991)
Sex Crime in the News. London, Routledge

Strange, Carolyn and Tina Loo (2002)
"From Hewers of Wood to Producers of Pulp: True Crime in Canadian Pulp Magazines of the 1940s," *Journal of Canadian Studies* vol. 37, 2, 11-32

Strange, Carolyn and Tina Loo (2002)
"The Moral of the Story: Gender and Crime in Canadian True Crime Magazines of the 1940s," in Thornton, Margaret, ed., *Romancing the Tomes: Feminism, Law, and Popular Culture.* London: Cavendish

Striker, Susan (2001)
Queer Pulp: Perverted Passions from the Golden Age of the Paperback. San Francisco, Chronicle Books

Surette, Ray (1998)
"Some Unpopular Thoughts about Popular Culture," in Bailey, Frankie Y. and Hale, Donna C. (eds.) *Popular Culture, Crime, and Justice.* London, Wadsworth

Vicarel, Jo Ann (1995)
A Reader's Guide to the Police Procedural. New York, G. K. Hall

Walden, Keith (1982)
Visions of Order. Toronto, Butterworths

Wallace, W. Stewart (1931)
Murders and Mysteries, a Canadian Series. Toronto, Macmillan

ABOUT THE AUTHORS

 **CAROLYN STRANGE** (sometimes known as "Dr. Death") has written extensively about the history of murder and capital punishment in Canada, the U.S. and Australia. With Tina Loo and others, she coordinated a project on prison history tourism at Robben Island, Port Arthur, and Alcatraz. Much of her work has focussed on the sometimes-curious connections between crime and popular culture. She teaches criminal justice history at the University of Toronto (when she isn't watching film noir classics and *Law & Order* reruns).

 When she isn't on the lam in the high arctic, **TINA LOO** (a.k.a. "Doc Holiday") teaches Canadian history at the University of British Columbia, where she specializes in cultural and environmental history. With Carolyn Strange, she has explored the strange and ironic world of crime and popular culture, looking at prison tourism on Alcatraz Island, the circus, and, of course, pulp magazines.